T0210907

Misinformation Matters

What is "misinformation"? Why does it matter? How does it spread on the internet, especially on social media platforms? What can we do to counteract the worst of its effects? Can we counteract its effects now that it is ubiquitous? These are the questions we answer in this book. We are living in an information age (specifically an "algorithmic age") which prioritizes information "quantity" over "quality." Social media has brought billions of people from across the world together online and the impact of diverse platforms, such as Facebook, WeChat, Reddit, LinkedIn, Signal, WhatsApp, Gab, Instagram, Telegram, and Snapchat, has been transformational.

The internet was created, with the best of intentions, as an online space where written content could be created, consumed and diffused without any real intermediary. This empowering aspect of the web is still, mostly, a force for good. People, on the whole, are better informed and online discussion is more inclusive because barriers to participation are reduced. As activity online has grown, however, an expanding catalogue of research reveals a darker side to social media, and the internet generally. Namely, misinformation's ability to negatively influence our behaviour both online and offline.

The solution we provide to this growing dilemma is informed by Ludwig Wittgenstein's *Tractatus Logico-Philosophicus*, which examines the relationship between language and reality from a philosophical perspective, and complements Claude Shannon's Information Quantity Theory, which addresses the quantification, storage, and communication of digital information from a mathematical perspective. The book ends by setting out a model designed by us: a "Wittgensteinian" approach to information quality. It defines content published online by clarifying the propositions and claims made within it. Our model's online information quality check allows users to effectively analyse the quality of trending online content. This approach to misinformation analysis and prevention has been designed to be both easy to use and pragmatic. It upholds freedom of speech online while using the "harm principle" to categorise problematic content.

MISINFORMATION MATTERS

Online Content and Quality Analysis

Uyiosa Omoregie
Kirsti Ryall

CRC Press
Taylor & Francis Group
Boca Raton New York London

CRC Press is an imprint of the
Taylor & Francis Group, an **informa** business

First edition published 2023
by CRC Press
6000 Broken Sound Parkway NW, Suite 300, Boca Raton, FL 33487-2742

and by CRC Press
4 Park Square, Milton Park, Abingdon, Oxon, OX14 4RN

CRC Press is an imprint of Taylor & Francis Group, LLC

Library of Congress Cataloging-in-Publication Data
Library of Congress Cataloging-in-Publication Data
Names: Omoregie, Uyiosa, author. | Ryall, Kirsti, author.
Title: Misinformation matters : online content and quality analysis / Uyiosa Omoregie, Kirsti Ryall.
Description: First edition. | Boca Raton : CRC Press, 2023. | Includes bibliographical references and index.
Identifiers: LCCN 2022048220 (print) | LCCN 2022048221 (ebook) | ISBN 9781032311555 (hardback) | ISBN 9781032311562 (paperback) | ISBN 9781003308348 (ebook)
Subjects: LCSH: Social media. | Misinformation. | Information literacy.
Classification: LCC HM742 .O467 2023 (print) | LCC HM742 (ebook) | DDC 302.23/1--dc23/eng/20230110
LC record available at https://lccn.loc.gov/2022048220
LC ebook record available at https://lccn.loc.gov/2022048221

ISBN: 978-1-032-31155-5 (hbk)
ISBN: 978-1-032-31156-2 (pbk)
ISBN: 978-1-003-30834-8 (ebk)

DOI: 10.1201/9781003308348

Typeset in Caslon
by SPi Technologies India Pvt Ltd (Straive)

Contents

CONTENTS

Preface

The study presented in this short monograph began in the early months of the COVID-19 pandemic in 2020. Via social media, we received an avalanche of misinformation and personal messages on the subject of the virus, the pandemic, treatments, and government/ state responses from a number of friends, acquaintances, colleagues and relatives. This kick-started an ongoing conversation online between the two of us about the problems caused by the rapid spread of misinformation. Which, in turn, segued into our throwing back and forth possible ways of counteracting misinformation without it always ending up in online arguments and lectures, none of which are ever that successful. At least, not in our experience. Eventually, we came up with the idea of creating a simple checklist for social media users to help them better screen content received and filter out misinformation.

The internet is a place where online written content can be created, consumed and diffused without any real intermediary. The World Wide Web (the web) was conceived and designed originally as a plat-form that "should remain an open standard for all to use and that no-one should lock it up into a proprietary system" (CERN 2022). This empowering aspect of the web is generally a force for good.

Central to this monograph are two concepts: information *quantity* theory, brilliantly espoused by Claude Shannon (father of the information age), balanced by an approach to information *quality*, designed by us, and inspired by the work of Ludwig Wittgenstein.

We propose a framework for online misinformation analysis and provide a tentative online information quality theory. The concept of "algorithmic choice" for the rating and ranking of content for social media users is endorsed as a way forward. We also introduce our two new concepts: **non-information** and **off-information** which we believe are useful additional categories for labelling certain problematic content found online, in addition to the general categories of **misinformation, disinformation** and **malinformation**.

In the appendix to this monograph, we present the results of a qualitative online questionnaire administered to 81 social media users in Canada, the United Kingdom and Nigeria. The survey explores social media users' perception of the quality of information online and attitudes towards fact-checking and the forwarding of online content to other users. It was conducted over a period of two months between 25 September 2021 and 25 November 2021.

Nearly all respondents use online social media every day (95%): only 5% rarely use it. A large proportion of the respondents (72%) state that when sent news or information online, they have forwarded such content to others after reading only the headlines. Just over half (55%) state that they have encountered fact-checking websites/ apps, but most (84%) believe online fact-checkers/apps are important or necessary. About half of the respondents (53%) indicate that they would read content labelled by an independent analyst as "high quality," and a majority (70%) would forward or consider forwarding such content to others. If they encountered content labelled as "low quality," 63% of respondents would not forward such content to others.

While a small survey, it was, for us, important because it indicated that we were onto something important. It motivated us to move from our conversations and musings online, however interesting and enjoyable, and gave us the confidence to take the "wouldn't it be good if there was some sort of easy checklist" idea and research and develop it further. The results of which you're now reading.

We cannot guarantee our proposed system will persuade everyone using it that the incorrect content they have read should be questioned further. Nor can we state that everyone introduced to our system will choose to use it. We can all cling to beliefs and information that are partly or wholly untrue, even more so, sometimes, when we are presented with overwhelming evidence that we are wrong. What we hope though is that, for those who choose to use it, our system will become a handy method of sifting the wheat from the chaff while interacting with others online: that after a while it will become almost second nature.

About the Authors

The authors are the co-founders of Avram Turing, a research organisation focused on misinformation prevention and content analysis online.

Uyiosa Omoregie is the principal analyst at Avram Turing. He attended West Buckland School in England, UK. He is an alumnus of the University of London (The London School of Economics as lead college). He is a member of the Association of Internet Researchers (AoIR), the Canadian Association for Information Science and the Canadian Academy of Independent Scholars. He is a referee for the *Journal of Information Science* (SAGE Publishing) and *Misinformation Review* (Harvard University).

Kirsti Ryall is the principal researcher at Avram Turing. She attended West Buckland School in England, UK. She holds a degree in English Literature. She previously worked in advertising, marketing, and fundraising roles as a graphic designer, copywriter, proof-reader, and as a trainer helping others on how best to present their work. She is a member of the Association of Internet Researchers (AoIR).

1

INTRODUCTION

Billions of people from around the world connect with one another online via social media. It is in no way hyperbolic to compare how the internet, and in particular social media, has transformed the way we interact and share information at all hours of the day with the way in which the invention of the printing press transformed on a global level the ease and speed with which people were able to access the written word and share information.

The number of active users of the six most popular online social networks combined is estimated at about 10 billion (Statista 2022). The general absence of a legally recognised, global infrastructure of intermediaries online has allowed the development of a "free-for-all" direct path from the producers of questionable content to consumers. And in recent years, two disturbing trends have been highlighted: "information disorder" and "echo chambers."

Online Platforms' Existential Crisis

The World Economic Forum highlighted "information disorder" as a threat to society (World Economic Forum 2018). There are now online spaces ("echo chambers") in which people are only exposed to content created or shared by like-minded users of the platform. Similar to "echo chambers" are "filter bubbles," spaces created artificially by "algorithms" harnessing a user's online history to make further suggestions or content recommendations that may be of interest. Echo chambers and filter bubbles reduce the quality of discourse online and can directly and indirectly lead to the creation and diffusion of biased and unsubstantiated content. This is particularly true when people do not recognise that the information they are accessing online has been processed in this way.

What this means in practice is that a person can read information online and gradually have less and less information from

DOI: 10.1201/9781003308348-1

other viewpoints highlighted by the filter bubble's algorithms. Understandably, that person may well continue to believe that the information they are accessing is unfiltered, only to end up having difficult, contentious conversations both on and offline with colleagues, friends or family who are accessing *their* online information from within a different filter bubble. The person believes that they are seeing the same information online as others and cannot comprehend why their friends, relatives or colleagues refuse to consider, let alone believe, the "truths" the person has been reading, thanks to their filter bubble's algorithms.

It is human nature that most of us, if we feel we are being dismissed as liars, or as being naive or stupid, will, a lot of the time, double down on what we believe to be the "truth." From there, it is all too easy for us to move from accessing information within the filter bubble surrounding us, created by algorithms, to seeking out places where we can chat and share opinions with like-minded people. Places where we can spend time with people who we feel are on our wavelength: people who aren't constantly questioning us or telling us we're wrong. Especially when the algorithms that have created and continue to refine our filter bubble end up suggesting and recommending such forums, groups and organisations, thereby facilitating our move from filter bubble to echo chamber.

While nowadays people are more likely to have heard about algorithms and echo chambers than a few short years ago, it cannot be assumed that this translates into a full understanding of just how great a difference algorithms make to the information being filtered through to the online user. Nor just how ubiquitous algorithms are in our daily life. Businesses and corporations often portray algorithms as doing little more than reproducing in the online world the ways in which advertisements are selected and placed in print publications. Or the ways in which advertisers select which versions of which advertisements will be placed on different TV channels, depending on the time and the programmes that the ad breaks wrap around. We are told that this is merely the same old way of tailoring advertisements to an expected particular audience. All that has changed is the media in which the advertising appears.

The difference is, however, that while the historical versions (surveys of different sections of society; previewing advertisements with focus groups; using sales figures and other statistics to ascertain who is purchasing items and from where) of today's algorithms enabled companies to adjust their tone, vocabulary, emphasis, and selection of advertising slots to better fit a specific audience, readers/viewers were still very much aware that other products existed. They would see and hear either the same product being marketed slightly differently on different platforms (magazines, newspapers, TV and radio channels) or different but similar products being promoted.

There was little or no attempt by the advertiser to prevent anyone from even getting to see other advertisements, or to make it near impossible for someone to access information about other companies' products unless they set out deliberately to access the products. This might seem an inconsequential thing when viewed purely as an interaction between an advertiser and their potential audience. Take into account how this interaction works between a group (or person or publication) seeking to proclaim their "truth" as the real version of events and someone browsing online, across various social media platforms and websites, and the interaction becomes more dangerous.

A foundation of facts secures any civilisation. False information online usually serves one of two purposes, often both: for clickbait (to draw attention and hence attract web traffic for financial gain) or in order to influence/mould beliefs and major events. As society has become more aware of the spread of false information online, three different responses to the problem of information disorder and echo chambers have been applied.

The initial response was to do nothing and leave consumers free to discern content, and its authenticity, for themselves. It was argued the web was a place for free expression and that online liberty should not be stifled (McCarthy 2020).[1] As misinformation became more widespread online, the next response was to censor harmful content – with the removal of content that was deemed unfit for public consumption (Business Standard 2021).[2] More recently, various third-party actors have created websites that use a set of criteria to fact-check trending online content or certify the credibility (trustworthiness) of popular online news websites. And social media platforms have begun fact-checking what is posted and shared on their sites by users. Though the jury is still out on how vigorously and successfully they do this.

These third-party arbiters of truth and credibility use prescriptive tools to help sanitise online content. Research has, however, revealed the limitations of fact-checking as a misinformation prevention strategy (Cook et al. 2017). When deeply held beliefs are involved, providing "facts" alone may not change beliefs. Sometimes, the opposite effect of strengthening the false belief occurs. This has led to the strategy of trying to prevent or neutralise misinformation through "inoculation" or "prebunking" (Brashier et al. 2021).

When asked about misinformation online, Alan Rusbridger commented, "In a world of information chaos, when people don't know what is true and what is untrue and who to trust about information, society becomes unworkable" (Sakur 2021). Rusbridger, the former editor-in-chief of the Guardian newspaper (UK), current Chair of the Reuters Institute for the Study of Journalism, and serves on the Board of the Committee to Protect Journalists. He is now a member of Facebook's "oversight board" and makes important decisions on the moderation of content on the platform.

Facebook, Twitter, YouTube, Parler, WhatsApp, and other global online public communications platforms are facing a content moderation crisis. As Christopher Mims, the tech writer for the Wall Street Journal, puts it, the two questions challenging these online platforms are "How do we make sure we're not facilitating misinformation, violence, fraud or hate speech? At the same time, how do we ensure we're not censoring users?" (Mims 2021). How, in fact, can we find a way of balancing these two apparently opposite concerns to most benefit the greatest number of people?

One analyst summarises the power and pain of the internet this way:

> The popularization of the Internet must be one of the greatest human discoveries, to be put on par with those of language, writing and printing. This discovery opens up the possibility to improve the collective human intelligence with the power of billions of individual intelligences. However, it should be noted that collective intelligence evolves much more slowly than that of individuals, and that it always remains much lower than that of "certain" individuals. The Internet has also weaknesses that may just reverse all its positive qualities into negative, perhaps even fatal, defects. This is because, like any other human creation, it can be controlled or manipulated by "some" humans, that may

use it to support "their" own interests, at the expense of the entire humanity. Being aware of the problem is certainly the most actual and important thing to do in the current times.

(Debest 2021 discussion with Uyiosa Omoregie)

Economic Impact of Misinformation

On 23 April 2013 the Associated Press (AP) Twitter account sent out false information (Selyukh 2013). The tweet stated falsely that an explosion in the White House had injured the US President Barack Obama. This AP Twitter page was actually hacked. The act of misinformation (more specifically, disinformation) caused the Dow to drop by 200 points, with a temporary loss of value ($136.5 billion) from the S&P 500 index.

Misinformation online (especially "fake news") costs the global economy about $80 billion annually. Each year the global stock markets are impacted negatively by misinformation to the tune of about $40 billion. Annually, the market value of global stock markets is vulnerable to a 0.05% loss due to fake news. The retirement savings sector in the USA suffers about $19 billion annually from deliberate financial misinformation. These startling numbers were revealed in a report by the University of Baltimore and the cybersecurity company CHEQ (University of Baltimore/CHEQ 2019).

This research discovered the "price paid in the form of both direct and indirect costs which collectively undermine the cardinal principle of trust that underpins market economies" (University of Baltimore/CHEQ 2019, p. 3). It showed that misinformation affects negatively myriad industries: healthcare, reputation management, stock markets, the media, election campaigns, and financial information, to name a few.

The researchers also discovered that the power of online presence can be bought too, enabling misinformation to be targeted in order to positively or negatively influence people's behaviours and decisions. A social media account with more than 250,000 followers costs about $2500. Apparently, $55,000 could fund an attack on Twitter to discredit a journalist. The outcome of a national referendum, trade agreements, country elections and national policies all could be influenced online with enough funding (approx. $400,000) (University of Baltimore/CHEQ 2019, p. 4).

Falsehood Travels Fast

The 23 April 2013 Associated Press (AP) hack incident was a show-case for the speed and virality of falsehoods online. Within seconds, the misinformation with critical national security implications was retweeted hundreds of times, with the potential to reach millions of people within hours. These are the two most troubling aspects of mis-information online – speed and reach. One study discovered that on the Twitter platform, untruthful content was retweeted quicker, and by more people (any retweets by bots were stripped out of the data set), than truthful content, with 70% more retweets (Vosoughi et al. 2018). In the researchers' own words, the findings left them, "some-where between surprised and stunned" (MIT News 2018). It took six times longer for true stories to reach 1500 people as it did false stories, with false stories reaching a Twitter cascade (an unbroken retweet chain) of ten around twenty 20 times faster than stories that were factually correct: tweets about political news being by far the largest category (MIT News 2018).

The fact that it is human behaviour, rather than bots' activity, that is responsible for spreading the majority of false news, whether by design or in good faith on the part of the retweeter, suggests that better education, at all ages, of what misinformation is and how to recognise its various forms is more likely to make a difference to the problem than relying solely on technological solutions. Something that the MIT study's authors point out. If people are spreading false news – whether deliberately or unwittingly – such activity will be counteracted better using multiple solutions including the creation of "measurements or indicators…[that] could become benchmarks" (MIT News 2018).

The Algorithmic Age

The twenty-first century, with the advent of Web 2.0, launched humanity into the algorithmic age. We no longer live in just the computer age: algorithms now take centre-stage in all the advanced technologies we have, quite literally, at our fingertips every day. Algorithms have become indispensable to our daily lives to an extent that most of us have little idea and even less understanding. Whether it is voice recognition on our phones; using Google to translate from one language to another; Netflix and other streaming providers suggesting new movies or shows to watch, based on our previous viewing choices; or the ability to speak to our phones directly and ask it to show us the nearest bus stop, restaurant, or cinema, we now rely on algorithms in a way that would have seemed incomprehensible to us even 10 to 15 years ago.

An algorithm is basically a set of instructions. It's a recipe, a step-by-step procedure that takes inputs to process output. These steps are mathematical and are used as a means of rapidly processing large amounts of data. Algorithms are configured mostly for automated reasoning and decision-making. They're designed to speed up processes that would otherwise hold things up and add to the time a consumer/customer has to wait, thus increasing the possibility they will become bored, frustrated, or run out of time. Or they measure the amount of time ("Dwell Time") that we spend looking at something online having clicked on a link or post, and then use that information to dictate the order in which each of us sees similar items going forward. The pleasure of algorithms is that they can help us to enjoy more personalised experiences online. The pain of algorithms is that they can amplify problematic content or even release output that is biased or discriminatory (Noble 2018). Algorithms are not perfect because humans are not perfect. And, it is humans who are responsible for the creation of algorithms. With all of our conscious and unconscious biases. With all of our foibles and weaknesses.

Just as a recipe and each of its step-by-step instructions are only ever as good as the creator of that recipe, so it is with the algorithm. In the case of recipes, if, having tasted the results, we realise an ingredient has been omitted or given an incorrect amount, we can amend the recipe to work better or do not bother making it again. We don't have that option with the incorrect algorithm. Well, not unless we are a skilled coder who sees the bias in an algorithm, understands how that bias has affected the algorithm's design, and either works for the company that created the algorithm or is well-known and respected enough to know that if they say something publicly people will listen.

The additional danger with algorithms, however, is that we may not even realise that an algorithm is the reason why our job application may have been rejected – because of an automated screening process. Or the reason our insurance policy is much higher than we expected – because the perceived risk to our property, vehicle and possessions has been calculated based on where we live, our name and our level of education. We may be unaware that algorithms can affect the chances of our facial profiles being identified correctly, depending on the colour of our skin (Buolamwini and Gebru 2018, pp. 1–15). Or that the types of political information directed our way are the result of algorithms that have crunched all the data available online about our income, geography, job, comments and posts on social media and used it to calculate what content is more likely to capture our interest and increase the time we spend on a specific website or social media platform.

We may have some vague understanding that these algorithms are based on all the personal details we have placed willingly, or unwittingly, online over several years, yet possess little comprehension of just how easy it is to collate all the disparate facts and opinions we have proffered up online. Or, we may have no knowledge at all of what an algorithm is and how it affects what we do online.

Harari (2017) argues that data reigns supreme today and its power can be compared to the power held by religion or political philosophy in the last century. **Dataism** is the belief that the world today consists of data flows and the intrinsic value of any object or being is the data it holds or brings. "Dataists" may regard the human species simply as a data-processing system (individual people as microchips) to be mined and exploited. Technological determinism is another way to describe the present algorithmic age, as Verdegem argues:

> We are entering a new era of technological determinism and solutionism in which governments and business actors are seeking data-driven change, assuming that Artificial Intelligence (AI) is now inevitable and ubiquitous. But we have not even started asking the right questions, let alone developed an understanding of the consequences. Urgently needed is debate that asks and answers fundamental questions about power.
>
> *(2021 email to Uyiosa Omoregie)*

Whatever the terminology, the rapid spread of the internet following its conception means that the power contained within the combination of our freely given personal data and algorithms is something the vast majority of the world is yet to fully understand. And we include ourselves in that camp! Add that to the fact that the creator of an algorithm can all too easily incorporate their own conscious or unconscious bias into the algorithm (the equivalent to that missing ingredient or getting the ingredient ratios in a recipe slightly wrong in our recipe analogy) and the result can be, and has been, a very real damage to people's lives.

Computationalism

The twenty-first century is a time during which, according to Golumba (2009), the ubiquitous trust in the power of computers has morphed into an overarching ideology and belief-system that he calls "computationalism." By computationalism, Golumba means "a commitment to the view that a great deal, perhaps all, of human and social experience can be explained via computational processes" (2009, p. 8). Golumba views computationalism as a problematic ideology because of its strong links with technological corporations' hegemony and surveillance systems. Clark and Chalmers (1998, pp. 7–19) go further and suggest that computers are part of the "extended mind" of humans today. They begin their famous paper with the question: "Where does the mind stop and the world begin?" The normal answer to the question is that the mind stops in the brain inside the human skull. Clark and Chalmers think not: they believe that artefacts external to the human brain (like notebooks, diaries and more importantly computers) can contain aspects of a human's thought and memory. Our laptops, smartphones and Facebook profiles are parts of our overall cognitive system. Clark famously credits this insight to the day he forgot to take his laptop with him on a journey. Without his laptop, Clark felt like a part of his brain was missing. In his most recent book, Chalmers is careful to clarify that the extended mind hypothesis is not an argument that human consciousness is something that can be extended or outsourced to an external artefact (Chalmers 2022, p. 303).

Is the world made up of information? It was estimated that in 2007 the world's capacity to store technological information (technical capacity) was 2.9×1020 optimally compressed bytes (Hilbert and

Lopez 2011, pp. 60–65). That's a lot of information. Wittgenstein's book *Tractatus Logico-Philosophicus* could be interpreted as making a case that the world is made of facts, hence information: "The world is a totality of facts, not of things" (Wittgenstein 1922, p. 21). Shannon coined the term "bit" binary digit, in his landmark paper (1948, pp. 379–423, 623–656), but the concept of the binary as a fundamental structuring of the world dates back to ancient times. As Chalmers reveals, the ancient philosopher Pythagoras in 550 BCE believed that the world was made up of numbers. Ancient African (*Ifá*) and Chinese (*I Ching*) divination systems are based on binary patterns. Leibniz was actually influenced by the *I Ching* when he invented the modern binary system in the eighteenth century that is still the foundation of digital computation today (Chalmers 2022, pp. 145–146).

Notes

1 It can be argued that if serious concerns about misinformation were raised from the beginning of the internet age (roughly 25 years ago), social media would not have developed as fast as it did. Freedom of expression, paramount from the beginning, made social media to develop rapidly and permeate the world.
2 Censoring of content (especially political content) can be controversial. The censoring of the Nigerian President by Twitter and retaliation by the President against Twitter was headline news. For a balanced and insightful analysis see article by Nwauabi: https://www.bbc.com/news/world-africa-58175708.

2

BACKGROUND

A Brief History of Falsehood Propagation

Misinformation propagation in its current form is a global problem that requires urgent solutions. It is not, however, a new problem. Historically, instances of misinformation being circulated in the public arena can be found as far back as the sixth century CE. For example, misinformation was propagated publicly when Procopius, the historian, wrote deliberate falsehoods to tarnish the image of Emperor Justinian (Darnton 2017). In the history of misinformation propagation, three periods are generally recognised by scholars as turning points: World War II, the Cold War, and the 2016 presidential elections in the United States of America (Freedland 2020; Kreiss 2021; Marwick et al. 2021).[1]

Anstead (2021) provides a history of information and misinformation, starting from the medieval world. He shows that even prior to the medieval world, most seismic events in Roman history were flavoured or instigated by libellous stories. Historically, from medieval times to the present day, certain patterns in the construction and propagation of misinformation can be seen. What makes medieval times different from the present day is the nature of the society at the time: the "institutions" prevalent and notions of power and authority. Many of the most potent (and global) types of prejudices against certain races propagated today first had their seeds sown through misinformation propagation in the Middle Ages. A particular example is misinformation in the thirteenth century about "blood libel" and Jews in England that led to Edward I being expelled. This antisemitic misinformation flowed through the centuries, became more developed in the twentieth century and is still manifest today, especially in far-right ideology/conspiracy theories and extremist hate groups.

The Invention of the Printing Press and (Mis)information Propagation

The invention of the printing press in the Middle Ages was critical for the Reformation in the sixteenth century: the printing press ensured that texts were widely available, and the flow of information in the world has not stopped since. Not only the Reformation, but key intellectual revolutions like the Renaissance and the Enlightenment would not have happened without the printing press (Eisenstein 1980). With the printing press, the monopoly of ideas held by the ruling class or elites was broken and the democratisation of publishing began. According to Anstead (2021, p. 17), an estimated three million plus books were published in the year 1550: this single year produced more books than in the whole of the fourteenth century CE. This democratisation of publishing led to not only increased literacy but also increased propagation of misinformation.

From Mass Media to Fragmented Media

Anstead (2021) suggests that the world has now moved from an era of mass media to a new era dominated by fragmented media. The era of mass media dominated by a relatively small number of newspapers, television and radio was one with tight controls, regulations and monopoly of broadcast content. The number of channels initially available on television and radio was very limited and programmes were broadcast at set times with no option for replay by the consumer. If you missed a programme you missed it. You either didn't hear about it, or you heard about it second hand (someone you knew told you about it, or you read a review of it in a newspaper). What didn't happen was that either you were able to look up the programme, click on it and watch it, or someone you knew sent you the link for you to watch it. The ability to share content quickly and easily just wasn't available. Newspapers were printed as daily editions; a reader would have to go to a bricks-and-mortar library to get an old paper edition of a newspaper (or a bit later on, look it up on microfiche, while in the library).

We now have a fragmented media "infosphere" where content is segmented, giving consumers more choice and control. Between 2013 and 2020 the number of people in 40 countries surveyed who received their news primarily from social media increased while consumption of print media decreased drastically. In the United Kingdom, people who received their daily news primarily from television declined by about 25%. The same survey also found a 37% decrease in print media consumption in the United Kingdom (Anstead 2021, p. 33).

As the media infosphere became more fragmented, the print media began copying the tricks that online media platforms were using. In addition to setting up online versions of their print media, newspapers changed the ways in which they wrote. Headlines became more dramatic. Content, while still factual, began to have an increased amount of opinion included in articles (and increasing amounts of opinion from members of the public as well as that of people considered experts in a specific field). Print news publications now contain more sensationalist, divisive language than in previous eras because, as is the case online, it helps capture people's interest and increases the likelihood of them purchasing the publication (or at least increases their brand recognition and thus the potential for future interactions between the consumer and the publication – whether through their online or print formats). All of this enables news companies to convince advertisers that it is still worth their while to advertise with the company, either online, in print or in both formats. Something that is of greater importance as the number of faithful, long-term subscribers to specific newspapers reduces.

Social Media's Turn from Democracy to Authoritarianism

The democratisation of content production and consumption that a fragmented infosphere promised appears to have been short-lived. Analysts now lament how the internet is dominated by monopolies controlled by a handful of corporate organisations. Gehl (2014) notes that the "archival capacities of social media allows for new centralizations of power hidden away beneath the abstractions of the smooth, user friendly interfaces" (p. 15). Gehl further states that major social media corporations are now hegemonic with negative consequences for democracy. He calls this hegemony "new media capitalism" (p. 15):

> … it reduces online interaction to binary declarations of like-it-or-not consumer choices; it hides and inures us to the surveillance systems operating underneath its surface; it relies on the free labor of its users to build its content while the site owners make billions by selling user data and stock in their companies; its centralization (which always seems to be part of the political economy of capitalism, despite the repeated cries of creative destruction, disruption, innovation, and competition) provides an all-too-easy means by which states can gather data on citizens; and it promotes a culture of anxiety and immediacy over depth. In short, contemporary social media hardly seems compatible with democracy.…
>
> *(Gehl 2014, p. 65)*

Propaganda

Scholars began studying propaganda as a concept during World War II. "Disinformation" as a concept is a product of the Cold War and derives from the Russian word "dezinformatsiya." During the Cold War, state actors on both sides of the Iron Curtain engaged in misinformation propagation. What is distinctive about present-day misinformation propagation is the speed, reach and virality, amplified by online social media. During the 2016 US presidential elections, an estimated 126 million Americans were exposed to online content containing misinformation, sponsored by a foreign country (Ingram 2017).

And now, as we write this book (literally as the first proof of this section was being typed), we are seeing how Russia is using its state-run news channels, other media and social media to spread disinformation as Vladimir Putin seeks to persuade Russian citizens, and those further afield, that he is not invading Ukraine. Rather than war, according to him, he has instigated a "Special Operation" in order to rescue the citizens of Ukraine from their government. A government run by people he seeks to recast as a "bandit cabal" responsible for "genocide against ethnic Russians" in the contested Donbas region of Ukraine and "a gang of drug addicts and neo-Nazis, who occupied Kyiv and took the entire Ukrainian people hostage" (The Guardian 2022). These blatant lies are made yet worse directed as they are against Ukraine's democratically elected president, Volodymyr Zelenskyy, who is Jewish. A man whose relatives died in the holocaust. A man whose grandfather was the only one of four brothers to survive and who fought against the Nazis – as a soldier in the Soviet army. Russians are being denied access to social media and news sites reporting anything that does not seek to parrot the official Kremlin line.

Misinformation online (in this case deliberate, state-instigated misinformation) is having a very real effect in the real world, the repercussions of which are likely to be felt for a number of generations to come. It is contributing to a breakdown of familial relationships between those with relatives in both Russia and Ukraine. A not uncommon situation, especially close to the Russian/Ukrainian border, or for families where some relatives are living in the Donbas, Crimea and other places currently under the control of Russia and others are living in the parts of Ukraine still under Ukrainian control. It is also adding to the anguish of those Russian families who have heard nothing from their children (many still in their teens) who were told that as conscripts they would be taking part in military exercises (rather than being sent into a war zone), and continue to be told, if they are told anything at all, that all is well by the Russian military. Only for these same families to discover weeks later that their children are dead and were in fact killed several weeks earlier.

Further abroad, the daily misinformation being broadcast online by the Russian state is being used by those with an axe to grind against their own country's politicians and political parties, with little comprehension or concern about how their own broadcasts might then be used by the Russian state as a way of "confirming" to its citizens that what it is doing is right. That Russia uses their broadcasts to "prove" that, outside of specific western administrations, there are plenty of people who are questioning what Ukraine is doing, rather than Russia's behaviour. One only has to look at how commentators such as Tucker Carlson have had clips of their shows played repeatedly by Russian state media to see how this is helping to confirm as "true" the misinformation being broadcast within Russia (Thompson 2022). And how this links back to the misinformation spread online both in the 2016 and 2020 US election campaigns and during the Trump administration's time in office.

In this instance, we can see how easily misinformation produced by an individual, group or state for one reason is then be used by others as a means of confirming different misinformation, before being used (in a rather grotesque form of circularity) by the creator/s of the original misinformation to back up that misinformation – "[as] the narratives advanced by the Kremlin and by parts of conservative American media have converged in recent months, reinforcing and feeding each other" (Thompson 2022).

Crisis Discipline

The gravity of the information disorder challenge, and its effect on global collective behaviour, has led to calls for social media/information disorder to be designated a "crisis discipline" like medicine, conservation biology and climate science (Bak-Coleman et al. 2021). Just as Soulé (1985), conservation biologist and originator of the "crisis discipline" concept, argued originally in relation to his field of specialisation that, "[in] crisis disciplines one must act before knowing all the facts; crisis disciplines are thus a mixture of science and art, and their pursuit requires intuition as well as information" (pp. 727–734), so many now argue the same should be done when tackling the ever-increasing damage caused by online misinformation. In order to do that effectively, we need to define clearly the main causes of the problem, consider what it is possible to do to try and counteract the problem as much as possible, and create a system that can help us do so as easily as possible.

Note

1 Marwick et al. (2021) emphasise that disinformation was pervasive during the civil rights agitation era in the United States, the main difference now is that it is more widespread whereas in the middle of the last century it was more targeted against particular kinds of people.

3

A PHILOSOPHICAL
APPROACH

Facts, Belief, Opinion and Truth

Aphorisms abound, in the internet age, to help guide us through the digital jungle that's the World Wide Web. "Correlation is not causation" is one; another is "you are entitled to your opinions but not your own facts."

An "opinion" can belong to anyone without any consideration to "belief," "truth" or "fact" and it is always subjective.[1] "Belief" is also subjective and closely related to opinion – it is an acknowledgement of a state of affairs (real or unreal). "Truth," on the other hand, is less subjective and can be personal or generally believed by a group of people. "Truth" is less subjective than an opinion and is closely related to "fact." A "fact" is objective and not personal: it is generally believed by most people and supported with evidence. However, distinguishing "fact" from "truth" can be tricky. A colour-blind person sees a red ball but mistakes it for a purple one because of how their condition affects their perception of colour. For this colour-blind person, it is their "truth" that the ball is purple but the fact is that the ball is red. This is different from "alternative facts" or "alternative world-views."

Leibniz and Frege on "Truth" and "Fact"

Philosophers have long grappled with the concept of "truth" and "fact." Leibniz in his book *The Monadology* divides "truth" into two categories: truths of reasoning and truths of fact:

> There are also two sorts of truths: those of reasoning and those of fact. Truths of reasoning are necessary, and their opposite is impossible; those of fact are contingent, and their opposite is

DOI: 10.1201/9781003308348-3

possible. When a truth is necessary, we may discover the reason of it by analysis, resolving it into simpler ideas and truths, until we arrive at those which are ultimate.

(2016 [1714], p. 13)

Leibniz further states that "there are simple ideas of which no definition can be given...which cannot be proved" (2016 [1714], p. 13). For those "truths" that need justification, Frege divides them into two categories:

We divide all truths that require justification into two kinds: those for which the proof can be carried out purely by means of logic and those for which it must be supported by facts of experience.

(van Heijenoort 1967, pp. 1–82)

Frege posits that people make judgement calls whenever they acknowledge (or recognise) something to be true. Frege reveals the thought–truth–judgement––assertion connection:

(1) the apprehension of a thought – thinking,
(2) the recognition of the truth of a thought – judgement,
(3) the manifestation of this judgement – assertion.

(1959)

Frege further distinguishes between a "thing," an "idea" and a "thought":

One sees a thing, one has an idea, one apprehends or thinks a thought. When one apprehends or thinks a thought one does not create it but only comes to stand in a certain relation, which is different from seeing a thing or having an idea, to what already existed beforehand.

(1959)

Checking for "Truth" and "Fact" Online through Analysis

We (the authors of this monograph) further categorise online content as "analytical" if it is logical, coherent and contains claims supported by evidence. "Non-analytical" online content can be a mess of opinion, superstition, bias, prejudice and mere sentiments. Increasingly, more people choose to believe one point of view over another instead of choosing to carry outs some additional fact-checking when encountering an article online. The simple rule that we should read the whole piece before judging content and seek further information when necessary is being increasingly ignored. In our opinion, this is most likely due to people having too much faith that if something online looks "genuine" and coincides with their own beliefs and experiences it must be truthful. Or feeling overwhelmed by the sheer amount of content online and how easy it is to end up scrolling through various sites for hours or a combination of the two.

In this common scenario, it is easy to see how we can all end up using shortcuts, whether subconsciously or consciously, and decide we "know" enough to make a considered decision that what we are reading is true. And, having made that decision, be less inclined to then change our mind if someone else points out that we are wrong or condemns outright something we have chosen. We give greater weight to our decision by choosing to believe it is correct because we find that preferable to admitting we may have got our "facts" wrong.

That is why, for our online content analysis work, we have designed an analytical system that is descriptive and exploratory. It does not endorse or condemn articles online: it upholds freedom of speech. The rating (information quality) we give to the content we analyse is objective. Readers are given a more informed choice with which they can agree or disagree. Neither is it the case that our system's scoring cannot be reconsidered. It can and it should. New information in the future could reveal how truthful or not previously classified articles analysed using our system are now considered to be. In which case the scoring previously allocated to the content would be reconsidered. Our model has been designed so that, based on ongoing feedback and interaction, it can be adjusted to reflect such changes.

History is mutable: "facts" from the past can be discounted or broadened to include further research or new discoveries by people many years later. Our analytical checklist system is designed deliberately to not be prescriptive: to not be a ruling that insists readers should accept or reject an online article because we say so. Apparent "truths" and opinions change over longer periods of time. Take the example of the "lab leak" hypothesis of the origin of the COVID-19 virus. This hypothesis was dismissed and labelled initially as misinformation or as a conspiracy theory, in part because some of the groups spreading it were spreading other potentially dangerous conspiracy theories. However, with the passing of time, this particular hypothesis is now recognised as a plausible scenario that could explain how the virus spread, while the consensus at this time (based on research and data analysis) continues to be that the most likely scenario is the virus mutated as it spread from animal to human within one of the wet markets in the area.

Two of the simplest (and yet apparently so very difficult) things that humans can do are admit that they were wrong and that, knowing what they now know, they have changed their mind about what they believe. What was once viewed as general, normal and consensual can change as we learn more, as technology that might help us re-examine historical artefacts is created, and as society progresses.

The failure to set aside bias, prejudice and sentiments often cripples cognitive ability and distorts decision-making. In the subfield of management science known as decision theory or decision analysis, a "good" decision is differentiated from the "right" decision. It all has to do with information, objectivity and analysis. A good decision is a decision based on available evidence, data, information and analysis at the time the decision is made. It is generally not possible to know if a good decision will be the right decision until time and events say so. The right decision is simply a decision taken in the past that with hindsight turns out to be correct: the consequences of the decision are revealed as positive, predictive or the decision served the purpose of the decision-maker.

Decision and Action

We (the authors of this monograph) hold that opinions, beliefs, truths and facts are important to online content analysis if they can lead to knowledge (true or false), decision or action. This is in line with the "harm principle" that should guide interventions against certain categories of problematic content online. Action should only be taken against problematic content online if the content *can* cause harm. For content to have the potential to cause harm it must be able to lead to a harmful decision or action.

William James' Live/Dead Hypotheses

William James, in his 1896 paper *The Will to Believe*, differentiates a "live" hypothesis from a "dead" hypothesis. A hypothesis he defines as "anything that may be proposed to our belief." A "live" hypothesis contains an evident possibility when it is proposed but a "dead" hypothesis is completely unrealistic. James' pragmatic approach defines "belief" as a measure of a "willingness to act":

> ...deadness and liveness in an hypothesis are not intrinsic properties, but relations to the individual thinker. They are measured by his willingness to act. The maximum of liveness in an hypothesis means willingness to act irrevocably. Practically, that means belief; but there is some believing tendency wherever there is willingness to act at all.
>
> *(2014)*

Peirce also links belief to action:

> And what, then, is belief?...it has just three properties: First, it is something that we are aware of; second, it appeases the irritation of doubt; and, third, it involves the establishment in our nature of a rule of action.
>
> *(2020)*

W.V. Quine on Two Dogmas Obstructing Pragmatism

Quine describes two dogmas relating to "fact" and "truth" that must be abandoned for a more pragmatic focus in philosophy:

> One [dogma] is a belief in some fundamental cleavage between truths which are analytic, or grounded in meanings independently of matters of fact, and truths which are synthetic, or grounded in fact. The other dogma is reductionism: the belief that each meaningful statement is equivalent to some logical construct upon terms which refer to immediate experience. Both dogmas, I shall argue, are ill founded. One effect of abandoning them is, as we shall see, a blurring of the supposed boundary

between speculative metaphysics and natural science. Another effect is a shift toward pragmatism.

(1951)

Bertrand Russell's Scepticism

In his 1928 book, *Sceptical Essays*, Russell gives the following pragmatist commentary on "belief," "truth" and "fact":

> Although pragmatism may not contain ultimate philosophical truth, it has certain important merits. First, it realises that the truth that we can attain to is merely human truth, fallible and changeable like everything human. What lies outside the cycle of human occurrences is not truth, but fact (of certain kinds). Truth is a property of beliefs, and beliefs are psychical events. Moreover their relation to facts does not have the schematic simplicity which logic assumes; to have pointed this out is a second merit in pragmatism. Beliefs are vague and complex, pointing not to one precise fact, but to several vague regions of fact. Beliefs, therefore, unlike the schematic propositions of logic, are not sharply opposed as true or false, but are a blur of truth and falsehood; they are of varying shades of grey, never white or black. People who speak with reverence of the 'Truth' would do better to speak about Fact, and to realise that the reverend qualities to which they pay homage are not to be found in human beliefs. There are practical as well as theoretical advantages in this, since people persecute each other because they believe that they know the 'Truth'.

(2004, pp. 47–48)

Russell maintains a healthy scepticism (with a dose of pragmatism) in matters of science:

> I am prepared to admit any well-established result of science, not as certainly true, but as sufficiently probable to afford a basis of rational action.

(Russell, 2004, p. 2)

On the importance of the opinions of "experts," Russell states:

> ...the opinion of experts, when it is unanimous, must be accepted by non-experts as more likely to be right than the opposite opinion. The scepticism that I advocate amounts only to this: (1) that when the experts are agreed the opposite opinion cannot be held to be certain; (2) that when they are not agreed, no opinion can be regarded as certain by a non-expert; and (3) that when they all hold that no sufficient grounds for a positive opinion exist, the ordinary man would do well to suspend his judgement.
>
> *(2004, p. 2)*

Frank Ramsey's Principle

According to Ramsey, a person's belief is held to be true if it can lead to action. The success of the action guarantees the truth of the belief. This is a pragmatic conceptualisation of "belief." Ramsey emphasises that there are degrees of beliefs: partial or full. The degree of belief a person places on a proposition will reflect their willingness to act based on that belief. The more willing a person is to act, the higher the degree of belief. This is not so much about how strongly we feel about something, it is our level of conviction about the truth of a proposition that matters:

> ...for the beliefs which we hold most strongly are often accompanied by practically no feeling at all; no one feels strongly about things he takes for granted...the degree of a belief is a causal property of it, which we can express vaguely as the extent to which we are prepared to act on it. This is a generalization of the well-known view, that the differentia of belief lies in its causal efficacy...it is not asserted that a belief is an idea which does actually lead to action, but one which would lead to action in suitable circumstances; just as a lump of arsenic is called poisonous not because it actually has killed or will kill anyone, but because it would kill anyone if he ate it.
>
> *(Ramsey 2016)*

Ramsey further states the essence of his pragmatic approach:

> The essence of pragmatism I take to be this, that the meaning of a sentence is to be defined by reference to the actions to which asserting it would lead, or, more vaguely still, by its possible causes and effects. Of this I feel certain, but of nothing more definite.
>
> *(Ramsey and Moore 1927)*

Our emphasis on "decision" and "action" is very much Ramseyan and pragmatic. **Pragmatism**, in philosophy, is an approach that prioritises the success and practical applications of belief or opinion through analysis of its truth and meaning.

The Connection between Wittgenstein and Ramsey

Frank Ramsey was a genius who made ground-breaking and lasting contributions to the fields of philosophy, logic, mathematics and economics. What is especially impressive about Ramsey is that all his intellectual achievements were made by the time he died in 1930 at the young age of 26 years. Ramsey was recruited to translate Ludwig Wittgenstein's book *Tractatus Logico-Philosophicus* (TL-P) when he was a 19-year-old undergraduate at the University of Cambridge, England. In 1923, Ramsey's review of the TL-P was published in the philosophy journal *Mind*. That review is still generally regarded as the best short work of scholarship about Wittgenstein's book.

Ramsey was Wittgenstein's supervisor when Wittgenstein returned to Cambridge and submitted the TL-P as his PhD thesis, after spending many years away. Wittgenstein regarded Ramsey as his intellectual equal and credits him for revealing the flaws in the TL-P and as well as inspiring him in his work. Wittgenstein reveals this in the preface to his book *Philosophical Investigations* published in 1953:

> ...since I began to occupy myself with philosophy again, sixteen years ago, I could not but recognize grave mistakes in what I set out in that first book [TL-P]. I was helped to realize these mistakes - to a degree which I myself am hardly able to estimate - by the criticism which my ideas encountered from Frank Ramsey,

with whom I discussed them in innumerable conversations during the last two years of his life.

(1953, p. 4)

The feeling was mutual: Ramsey was inspired by Wittgenstein and
credits him in a paper published in 1927 in the *Proceedings of the
Aristotelian Society*:

> ...I must emphasise my indebtedness to Mr. Wittgenstein, from
> whom my view of logic is derived. Everything that I have said is
> due to him, except the parts which have a pragmatist tendency,
> which seem to me to be needed in order to fill up a gap in his
> system. But whatever may be thought of these additions of mine,
> and however this gap should be filled in, his conception of formal
> logic seems to me indubitably an enormous advance on that of
> any previous thinker.

(Ramsey and Moore 1927)

Philosophy of Information

Floridi describes the philosophy of information as a new area of
research: an enquiry into "the technological and informational framework within which we make sense of the world" (Warburton 2022).
He argues that from the time of Plato to Popper, the philosophy of
information has been a feature of philosophical thinking but only in
recent years has it been formalised into a subdiscipline in academia.
The philosophy of information has practical relevance for the internet
today in what Floridi describes as "a clash between two fundamental
ethical principles" (Warburton 2022): privacy and free speech online.

As Floridi explains, "you do a philosophy of information and try
to extract from that lessons that can inform your ethical discourse"
(Warburton 2022). Floridi is a philosophy of information professor,
but in 2014 he was given a role on Google's Advisory Council. His
remit was to provide "input, feedback, suggestions and recommendations" (Warburton 2022) on ethical issues for the company.

Our Own Model

When we began devising and refining our model, we both felt there was little point in coming up with solutions that would involve huge amounts of money (we don't have huge amounts of money) or a long period of time (things are already bad. We need a solution now, even if, ultimately, it is only an interim solution). We also agreed that the model we came up with should be one that could be adapted to different ages, different education levels, and one that would hopefully translate well across different cultures and communities.

While this monograph covers a lot of previous research, concepts and philosophical arguments, at its heart is, we hope, a clear, easy-to-understand-and-use model that will help the user better navigate the deluge of online articles, commentaries, news and "truths." That will help them become more confident in their ability to decide what is believable, what is not, and what needs to be investigated a bit more before making that decision.

So, where do we start?...

Note

1 We state that an opinion is always subjective because it is held by a person or when (collectively) one opinion is held by a group of people. Even if an opinion contains a fact, it is still subjective, only if a person states a fact directly is it not subjective but objective. We say truth is less subjective, using a scalar description, following Hodges (2001). Hodges quotes the ancient Greek Heraclitean philosopher, Cratylus: "It is impossible to say anything true about things that change" and suggests there could be borderline cases falling between truth and falsehood.

4

INTERVENTIONS

There are various types of interventions that are already being used to counteract the spread of misinformation online or that have the potential to be part of the solution in the future.

Content Moderation

Moderating content online requires transparency. Twitter and Facebook use a combination of machine learning and human analysts for content moderation. Twitter also publishes its content moderation processes and enforcement rules. A "behaviour-first approach" is used by Twitter which involves scrutinising the behaviour of a Twitter account first before reviewing content posted by the account (Dorsey 2020). It is vital for any systems moderating content online that the transparency they purport to uphold is truly transparent. Otherwise, the outcome may well be an increasing disbelief that such systems are genuinely transparent, leading in turn to people being more inclined to believe misinformation than they might have been previously. This is why various groups are calling for social media platforms' publishing of their content moderating to be regulated and required by law, rather than society relying on them to report their own activity. As was revealed in 2021, what is reported by a social media platform and what turns out to be the case can be very different.

"Prebunking" or inoculation involves exposing the flawed argumentation techniques of misinformation to prepare online content consumers against future misinformation. The importance of timing when correcting "fake news" has been emphasised in a study to demonstrate the effectiveness of debunking (Brashier et al. 2021). "Debunking" was defined as fact-checks after misinformation exposure, "labelling" (fact-checks of information presented during exposure) and "prebunking" (fact-checks before exposure).

DOI: 10.1201/9781003308348-4

"Tiplines" are fact-checks for content found on platforms with end-to-end encryption like WhatsApp. This novel solution uses crowd-sourced "tiplines" that contain "tips" submitted by users of a platform (when they encounter a forwarded message containing problematic content) that they feel should be fact-checked (Kazemi et al. 2021).

Content moderation at scale on a social media platform is not possible. "Brandolini's Law" (misinformation asymmetry principle) is an internet adage that states that the amount of effort needed to refute misinformation is of an order of magnitude more than that needed to produce the misinformation in the first place. The law was first stated in the form of a tweet in 2013 by Alberto Brandolini, an Italian computer programmer (Wikipedia: Brandolini's Law). Researchers have suggested that more effort should be focused on helping people to accept reliable information instead of attempting content moderation at scale (Acerbi et al. 2022).

Sharot (2021) suggests that greater incentives from social media platforms are required for online content consumers to engage more with "truth" online: more "carrots" are needed to complement "sticks." A visible high rating (such as that built into our content analysis system), denoting quality content, can act as a carrot, both for the creation of more quality content by those writing and posting online and for readers' increased engagement with such content. As Donovan (2020) emphasises, it is important that authoritative content is elevated online. The approach to misinformation prevention and analysis we present (the central premise of this monograph) achieves what Donovan describes by targeting the virality of content, something that is an ever-growing priority for social media platforms (Mims 2021).

Behavioural Nudges

Misinformation online becomes a challenge when it goes viral. Virality of content means the content is getting greater than normal engagement online: what is termed "amplification." Research has shown that nudging social media users to be more attentive to the content they share could help reduce misinformation propagation (Pennycook et al. 2021). Surveys and field experiments with Twitter users revealed that helping users pay more attention to the accuracy of online content increased the accuracy of content the users shared.

The researchers concluded that most social media users share misinformation online due to a lack of attention. More intuitive users who use their "gut feeling" when they encounter content online end up sharing more misinformation.

In 2020, Twitter began prompting people who were clicking to share articles without having read them to pause and read the article before sharing (while still leaving the final choice of what they did to the person). A similar "nudge," in response to the spread of misinformation on its platform, was when it began prompting users to comment on a tweet before retweeting it and encouraged users to quote tweets instead of retweeting. This intervention reduced the number of retweets on the Twitter platform by 25% (Dorsey 2020). The following year, in May 2021, Facebook followed suit. Previously, Facebook had added prompts if a person was sharing a link older than 90 days. It had also added pop-ups on posts that had been disputed by third-party fact-checkers. Facebook has also communicated its desire to rank content on its platforms differently, prioritising more valuable and informative content (Clegg 2021).

An intervention on TikTok, designed by behavioural scientists, helped reduce misinformation on the platform by 24% (Gosnell et al. 2021). The science behind this successful intervention is the insight that, psychologically, people are in either of two states: "hot states" or "cold states." When a social media user is in a cold state, thinking is more logical and deliberate compared with a hot state when users are more intuitive and emotional. Interventions that make users pause and think about what they want to share is critical for a fast-paced platform like TikTok.

Each of these small "nudges" had an effect on people's behaviour. Whether it was people opening articles and reading them before sharing/retweeting, choosing not to open an article and not to share/retweet, or having opened an article deciding not to share/retweet it, each small amount of "friction" translated into a not insignificant number of social media users rethinking their initial, immediate decisions (Social Media Today 2020). Another study revealed that social media algorithms can reduce the spread of misinformation by elevating ("up-ranking") content from trusted media websites, and "down-ranking" content from websites with low trustworthiness (low information quality) ratings (Pennycook et al. 2019).

Information Quality Ranking versus Algorithmic Ranking

Without some sort of "recommender" system or algorithmic curation of content in the internet (especially on search engines and in social media), the internet would be incredibly difficult to navigate. It is estimated that *every second*, on a social media site like Instagram, about 1000 posts are shared, on Facebook approximately 4000 photographs are uploaded, close to 6000 tweets are posted on the Twitter platform and users of the Snapchat platform share about 35,000 new snaps (Spectralplex 2022). Chayaka describes the present times as "an age of algorithmic anxiety" and asks the question:

> Interacting online today means being besieged by system-generated recommendations. Do we want what the machines tell us we want?
>
> *(Chayaka 2022)*

How Facebook's News Feed Works (Facebook 2021)

The News Feed is the first thing a user encounters on Facebook after each login. There are potentially thousands of different kinds of content that can appear on a user's News Feed, from friends and pages followed currently on Facebook to suggested pages and people to follow based on the user's previous interactions online. Without sorting these thousands of different items of content, the News Feed would not function properly. Facebook's News Feed algorithm uses four principles to sort and prioritise content for every user's News Feed:

1. **Inventory**: the whole set of content shared by other friends and pages followed.
2. **Signals**: thousands of signals like the user's internet speed or the time of posting the content.
3. **Predictions**: likelihood that the user will engage with the content.
4. **Score**: a relevancy score is a number given to each post to rank it.

Twitter's Switch to Algorithmic Ranking of Content

Twitter introduced an algorithmic ranking of content for a user's Twitter Feed Home in 2016. Prior to that, tweets on a user's wall were ranked in reverse chronological order. Twitter deploys a "personalised relevance model" prioritising some tweets over others based on content feature and engagement (Huzar et al. 2021).

Vanity Metrics and Quality Metrics

Metrics that focus solely on engagement by users can be called "vanity metrics" (Sipley 2021): the number of "likes," "forwards" to other users, etc. Quality metrics focus on the importance of the content: veracity, coherence, usefulness and so on.

Bridging-Based Ranking of Content

As an alternative to engagement-based or chronological ranking of content for users, a "bridging-based" ranking of content has been proposed (Ovada 2022). A bridging-based recommendation system would reward content shared online that bridges the ideological divide by ranking it higher than other content. Such ranking of content would potentially decrease social divisions online, when for example it elevates fact-based journalism over mere sensationalism.

Algorithmic Choice

The concept of "algorithmic choice" implies that social media users are able to decide what type of algorithm ranks content for them on the platform. Stephen Wolfram introduced this concept during a US Senate hearing in 2019, suggesting that online social media platforms should allow third-party companies to provide such algorithms. According to Wolfram, introducing market competition into algorithmic ranking of content would help to "de-monopolize automated content selection" (2019).

Receptive Reading and Participatory Restraint

Two social media literary practices that analysts think can help prevent echo chambers and the amplification of misinformation online are receptive reading and participatory restraint, defined thus:

Receptive reading occurs when a social media user wants to closely, and anonymously, read a commenting thread with the express purpose of understanding a divergent point of view. Participatory restraint is a strategic literacy practice whereby a social media user will purposely not respond to an inflammatory post because they want to limit the "oxygen of amplification" and contain the story…participatory restraint relies on a sophisticated understanding of the effects of amplification….

(Sipley 2021)

Media/Information/News/Digital Literacy

Educators and policymakers have often pointed to media literacy as a fundamental skill required by online content consumers to help prevent misinformation. It seems obvious that if a person can search properly for information online, if they can compare and contrast sources, then that person will be, to a large extent, better informed. This is mostly true. But what is more important is that media literacy skills must be developed together with critical thinking and analytical thinking skills. The ability to analyse content is more important than simply being better able to search for new information online.

Then there is the problem that Golebiewski and Boyd (2019) call "data voids." Search engines are now the primary tool utilised to find information about a topic, a term or an explanation. And search engines are not perfect, as they explain:

There are many search terms for which the available relevant data is limited, nonexistent, or deeply problematic. Recommender systems [like search engines] also struggle when there's little available data to recommend. We call these low-quality data situations "data voids"…low quality or low authority content because that's the only content available…These voids occur when obscure search queries have few results associated with them, making them ripe for exploitation by media manipulators with ideological, economic, or political agendas.

(2019)

Four types of "literacy" were identified by researchers for the information age (Anstead 2021, p. 64): "Media literacy" is about awareness of the distinct ideological or commercial agenda of some news media organisations which could influence how they report or produce news. "Information literacy" requires analytical and critical thinking skills when accessing, evaluating and making judgement about new information – especially information found online. Information literacy is "the ability to identify verified and reliable information, search databases, and identify opinion statements" (Sirlin et al. 2021). "News literacy" is concerned with how citizens engage with news in democratic societies, recognising that objective reporting of news may require value judgements. "Digital literacy" takes into consideration that the distinction between producers and consumers of news in the digital age is not always evident. Digital literacy has as its focus online content, the way it is produced and the special role that user-generated content now plays online. Of the four types of literacy, information literacy was found to be the most important for misinformation prevention.

Natural Language Processing, AI and Misinformation Prevention

Gottfried Leibniz (1646–1716), often described as "the last universal genius," envisioned a universal scientific language that would clarify thought (remove ambiguity and fallacies), expose logical falsehoods, solve all arguments and hence help mankind progress (Davis 2012, p. 12). This vision is sometimes referred to as "Leibniz's Dream." Such a dream realised today would necessitate a machine/algorithm able to filter out misinformation online. Not merely to filter out articles, posts, links, etc., that have previously been moderated and confirmed as containing misinformation, but able to respond in real time to posts.

Imagine typing this as a post on a friend's Facebook wall:

The world is flat

and immediately receiving this message from the platform's algorithm:

Error! MISINFORMATION

Or typing this:

Always keep a cobra or a deadly scorpion on your car seat

Only for the following to appear:

Error! OFFINFORMATION

Or, upon tweeting this:

The present King of the USA appointed his wife as Prime Minister in 2020

Twitter's algorithm replies:

Error! NONINFORMATION

GPT-3 Language Model

GPT-3 stands for Generative Pre-Trained Transformer 3. It's an artificial intelligence system, a language model capable of generating text of a quality similar to that generated by a human being. Johnson observes that GPT-3 can write "original prose with mind-boggling fluency – a development that could have profound implications for the future," and further states that "Siri and Alexa popularized the experience of conversing with machines, but this was on the next level, approaching a fluency that resembled science fiction" (Johnson 2022). Annette Zimmermann, a philosopher, explains the current hype about GPT:

> GPT-3, a powerful, 175 billion parameter language model developed recently by OpenAI, has been galvanizing public debate and controversy…Parts of the technology community hope (and fear) that GPT-3 could bring us one step closer to the hypothetical future possibility of human-like, highly sophisticated artificial general intelligence (AGI)…Why the hype? As is turns out, GPT-3 is unlike other natural language processing (NLP) systems, the latter of which often struggle with what comes comparatively easily to humans: performing entirely new language tasks based on a few simple instructions and examples. Instead, NLP systems usually have to be pre-trained on a large corpus

of text, and then fine-tuned in order to successfully perform a specific task. GPT-3, by contrast, does not require fine tuning of this kind: it seems to be able to perform a whole range of tasks reasonably well, from producing fiction, poetry, and press releases to functioning code, and from music, jokes, and technical manuals....

(Weinberg 2022)

Could GPT-3 be the AI system that can help moderate content online and combat misinformation? Don't believe the hype. Floridi, a philosopher of information, in a paper written with co-author Chiriatti, analysed the nature, scope, limits and consequences of this new AI technology. They used three tests (mathematical, semantic and ethical) and showed that GPT-3 failed because it was not designed to pass such tests. Instead of combating misinformation online, GPT-3 could actually do the opposite: flood the internet with problematic content.

In another paper written by 31 researchers and engineers, the authors praised GPT-3's ability to generate news articles indistinguishable from content written by humans, but they also detailed its potential harmful effects resulting from "potential misuse application" including misinformation, spam, phishing, and social engineering pretexting:

Any socially harmful activity that relies on generating text could be augmented by powerful language models. Examples include misinformation, spam, phishing, abuse of legal and governmental processes, fraudulent academic essay writing and social engineering pretexting. Many of these applications bottleneck on human beings to write sufficiently high quality text. Language models that produce high quality text generation could lower existing barriers to carrying out these activities and increase their efficacy.

(Brown et al. 2020)

Marcus insists that large language models like GPT-3 are not good models of human language because they cannot separate truth from fiction. Models like GPT-3 are good at predicting sequences of words and finding patterns in digital text, essentially by regurgitating data they have been trained on (billions of words). As Marcus explains, models like GPT-3 were not created with the intent to create misinformation but they will not be able to avoid misinformation:

> Fundamentally, GPT-3 is a model of *how words relate to one another*, not a model of *how language might relate to the perceived world*. Humans try to relate their language to what they know about the world; large language models don't. Which means the latter just aren't telling us much about the former.
>
> *(2022) [emphasis in the source]*

This is what one might describe as "syntax" versus "semantics." We could translate what Marcus is stating as the futility of trying to use syntactic means to solve semantic issues.

5

ANALYSING THE PROBLEM

Origins of Modern Logic and Language Processing Systems

Gottlob Frege (1848–1925) transformed the field of logic from what it had remained since the days of Aristotle and is regarded as the founder of modern logic and much of modern philosophy. Frege laid the foundations of predicate logic, first-order predicate calculus and quantificational logic – formal systems central to computer science and mathematics (also modern philosophy and linguistics). Independently, Charles Sanders Peirce also made foundational contributions similar to Frege's (Hammer 1998). Frege was stimulated by the ambiguity and imprecision of ordinary language and launched a project to overcome this hindrance. He did this by creating a new "formula language" with elaborate symbols and definite rules, focused more on conceptual content than rhetorical style. He called this formula language *Begriffsschrift* – a formal language for "pure thought" (van Heijenoort 1967). This *Begriffsschrift* and its use of quantified variables in sentences is a pillar of all systems of modern man-made computation and automation.

Before Frege, George Boole (1815–1864) created what later became known as "Boolean logic." Boole was concerned about "those universal laws of thought which are the basis of all reasoning, and which, whatever they may be as to their essence, are at least mathematical as to their form" (1952, p. 273). Boolean logic is the system behind the operations of modern computers. Claude Shannon applied Boolean logic (algebra) to solve problems using two symbols "1" and "0." This formulation first appeared in Shannon's 1937 master's thesis, "A Symbolic Analysis of Relay and Switching Circuits." This thesis is credited with launching modern switching theory – the foundation for digital computers today. It has been described as "possibly the most important, and also the most famous, master's thesis of the century" (MIT News 2001).

DOI: 10.1201/9781003308348-5

Our central hypothesis in this book is that "Wittgensteinian logic," applied in natural language processing technology, (if possible) via automation, could transform the quality of information online. Wittgensteinian logic, as described in this book, could help filter out inauthentic information (non-information, off-information, malinformation and misinformation) from content presented online (see Figure 5.1).

The Chomsky-Norvig Debate

The processing of human language by computers has been an important goal of informatics research from the beginning. This research challenge (artificial computing's capability to deal with the complexity of human language in an effective manner) has been described as the "Holy Grail" of the field (Bates 1995). Algorithms used by machine learning systems are a major focus of Natural Language Processing (NLP) research. There are generally two approaches: rules-based modelling and statistical modelling. Noam Chomsky transformed the field of linguistics with his rules-based approach and is a co-founder of the cognitive science field which has applications in Artificial Intelligence (AI), specifically NLP. Chomsky criticises the popular statistical approach to AI, specifically machine learning:

> It's true there's been a lot of work on trying to apply statistical models to various linguistic problems. I think there have been some successes, but a lot of failures. There is a notion of success ... which I think is novel in the history of science. It interprets success as approximating unanalyzed data.
>
> *(Norvig 2012)*

Chomsky argues that too great a focus on big data using statistical modelling will be bereft of explanatory insight – this is not the way science has traditionally been conducted. What is needed is to go beyond data mining and prediction to general principles about intelligent life, about cognition: these principles can serve as the basis for a science of artificial intelligence. However, Norvig, an artificial intelligence researcher devoted to a statistical modelling approach, disagrees with the rules-based approach favoured by Chomsky:

Statistical language systems are used successfully by hundreds of millions of people every day and have come to completely dominate the field of computational linguistics. For the first three decades, the field used techniques that were more in line with Chomsky's recommended approach, but starting in the mid-1980s, some researchers started to experiment with statistical models. Their success convinced over 90% of the researchers in the field to switch to statistical approaches.

(2012)

One way of looking at the Chomsky rules-based/Norvig statistical approach to the AI saga is as a conflict between engineering and science. "Good old-fashioned AI" was influenced by the formalisms introduced by Frege, whereas new AI is more influenced by big data and new technology (Kartz 2012). According to Chomsky, AI research has shifted its focus towards engineering with a lot of technological success. In so doing, however, this technological success has sacrificed the quest for understanding scientific principles and answering scientific questions in AI research. Chomsky believes the principles of AI research should be no different from other scientific investigations conducted in the theoretical manner pioneered by Galileo (Kartz 2012; Chomsky 2017).

To automate a misinformation filter based on Wittgensteinian Logic, like that described in Figure 5.1, a device/machine is required; a set of rules/quality check/algorithm capable of human-like reasoning. Pinker (1994) explains how English and other natural languages are "hopelessly unsuited to serve as our internal medium of computation" (pp. 69–72). Internal language "mentalese" for internal expression or thought is distinct from external expression through words (Pinker 1994, pp. 69–72). Carnap (1937) also laments the "unsystematic and logically imperfect structure" of natural languages (p. 2).

Other scholars have explained that communication (expression through words) is not the primary purpose of language. Instead, language is a distinct human instrument for the expression of thought (Everaert et al. 2015). "Thought" carries more information than "words" and the speaker may not be able to fully articulate to the receiver the full intentions of their thoughts through words alone: the receiver has to decode what they believe the speaker is trying to articulate (Pinker 1994, pp. 69–72). The challenges faced by a natural language, such as English, include: "ambiguity," "lack of logical explicitness," "co-reference," "deixis" and "synonymy" (Pinker 1994, pp. 69–72).

Wolfram also emphasises the connection between human thought and language as the major challenge for the development of natural language processing systems:

> By the 1980s it became clear – notably through the failure of attempts to automate natural language understanding and translation – that language cannot in most cases (with the possible exception of grammar-checking software) meaningfully be isolated from other aspects of human thinking.
>
> *(2002, p. 1104)*

AI Limitations and Prospects

Indeed, the whole concept of artificial "intelligence" could be called into question: one AI researcher, in discussion with Uyiosa Omoregie, believes that "automated decision-making" is a better description of what we today call artificial intelligence (Allington 2021). Baker argues that although AI has achieved success in tasks that most people regard as requiring high intelligence, like mastering chess, no AI system can today match a five-year-old child's mastery of the English language – a task most people regard as not requiring much intelligence (2001, p. 3).

We believe that the crux of our proposed Wittgensteinian approach to misinformation analysis is about making clear what is stated in online content. This is done by clarifying the propositions and claims in the written content. And, for the time being, only human analysts (not artificial intelligence) are capable of consistently and reliably filtering out inauthentic information from online content. This was made clear in the testimony to the US House of Representatives, by the Vice President of the online social media platform Facebook:

> We also use machine learning to assist in our fight against misinformation. Algorithms cannot fundamentally tell what content is true or false, but they do help in the process. Our machine

learning models use various signals to identify content which might be false or partly false. Comments expressing disbelief are one signal that helps inform our prediction, as well as feedback from our community when people mark something as false news.

(Bickert 2020)

Pearl (2018), one of the pioneers of AI who was at the forefront of research that led to statistical approaches to machine learning decades ago, believes that developing machines with human-like reasoning is possible. Pearl, like Chomsky, now urges researchers to focus more on teaching machines to use causal reasoning in addition to reasoning with association (statistical/probabilistic). Meanwhile, Wolfram envisions a future when "computational contracts" will govern social media, ensuring that platform policies, algorithms and user behaviour are aligned to an agreed set of rules:

In the past, things like legal contracts had to be written in English (or "legalese"). Somewhat inspired by blockchain smart contracts, we are now getting to the point where we can write automatically executable computational contracts not in human language but in computational language. And if we want to define constraints on the training sets or results of automated content selection, this is how we can do it.

(2019)

Father of the Information Age

Claude Shannon, the father of information theory, described a quantitative (mathematical) theory of communication. In Shannon's theory, the fundamental challenge for communication (and hence information) is the need for reproduction at one point of the exact or approximate message produced at another point (Shannon 1948). Shannon's theory led to technologies that encode, transmit, decode and store information. Technologies that are central to the information age.

The "meaning" of the information, however, was, for Shannon, a secondary issue. His mathematical theory of information was more about engineering than linguistics:

Frequently the messages have meaning; that is they refer to or are correlated according to some system with certain physical or conceptual entities. These semantic aspects of communication are irrelevant to the engineering problem. The significant aspect is that the actual message is one selected from a set of possible messages.

(1948)

Shannon introduced the concept of the "bit" or "binary digit" as a quantitative measure and unit of information. His theory was concerned with "the channel capacity" of information (data) transmission. An analogy would be designing a bus for a postman to carry letters and parcels: the content of the letters/parcels is irrelevant if you are only interested in providing a bus with the capacity to transport as many letters and parcels as possible from their start point (the sender of the letter/parcel) to their correct end point (the recipient of the letter/parcel).

Shannon's paper has been described as one of the "canonical readings" in the information science field (Brock and Amrute 2020). Chomsky argues that Shannon uses the term "information" in his paper in a narrow technical sense. In this technical sense, it does not matter whether the content transmitted by the communication channel is valid, misinformation or contradictory (Chomsky 2021 via email to Uyiosa Omoregie). This became problematic after Shannon's famous paper was published (Conway and Siegelman 2006, pp. 191–195). Carnap and Bar-Hillel (1952) call the exclusion of semantic aspects by Shannon a "theoretical restraint" and further explain that "great care has been taken to point out that this theory is not interested in the semantic aspects of communication."

Norbert Wiener is the founder of the field of cybernetics and his work influenced Shannon's paper. Unlike Shannon, Wiener emphasised semantic aspects as critical to cybernetics. Today, Wiener should be recognised as the co-founder of information theory. His work is gaining increasing relevance today as advances in machine learning emphasise the brain–machine interface mediated by information that Weiner envisioned in the 1940s (Nature Machine Intelligence 2019). Shannon cites Wiener's work in his paper, acknowledges his indebtedness to Wiener for "the basic philosophy and theory [of Shannon's paper]" and cites Wiener's paper as being the "first clear-cut formulation of communication theory as a statistical problem" (1948).

Information Quality Theory

Issues of information disorder online can be reduced to the issue of information *quality*. The algorithms built into some social media platforms play important roles in the virality of content online. Just as Shannon emphasised the *quantity* of information, so some of these algorithms appear more focused on the *quantity* of user engagement with content than the *quality* of the content and the engagement.

If, according to Shannon, the "semantic aspects" are irrelevant in the theoretical communication engineering solution (data transmission), then what really is "information"? Information scientists have adopted a General Definition of Information (GDI). According to the GDI, information is data that is well-formed and meaningful (Floridi 2019). Under this definition, misinformation and disinformation are not genuine information because they are false, although they may have semantic content. Semantic *factual* content is what distinguishes authentic information from false information, in declarative language (Floridi 2019; Levitin 2020, p. xv). Facts are central to any language: the primary use of language is to put forth facts or try to deny facts (Wittgenstein 1922, p. 4).

Information quality is chiefly an issue about meaning: the semantic aspects are more relevant than engineering efficiency or grammatical accuracy. A sentence can be grammatically correct but have no meaning, and an engineering solution can transmit more data quantity at the expense of information quality. Language functions properly only when it expresses meaning (Wittgenstein 1922). Chomsky, however, shows that the grammar of a language is really the theory of a language and is "autonomous and independent of meaning" (Chomsky 1957, p. 49). Chomsky further states:

> To understand a sentence, we must know much more than the analysis of this sentence on each linguistic level. We must also know the reference and meaning of the morphemes or words of which it is composed; naturally, grammar cannot be expected to be of much help here.

> *(1957, p. 49)*

Chomsky's famous examples to explain this are:

(1) *Colorless green ideas sleep furiously.*
(2) *Furious sleep ideas green colorless.*

Both sentences are meaningless, but the first is correct grammatically. Taken through our analytical filter, however (Figures 5.2 and 6.1), neither sentence would pass the information quality test. The two sentences have no semantic content and so, under our checklist, would be labelled "non-information." Likewise, in the examples mentioned in Table 5.1, all sentences are correct grammatically but only the fourth sentence contains authentic information. The first and second sentences are meaningless (non-information) and the third is a hypothesis (Wittgenstein 1922, p. 10).

Unless further evidence is given (or the presuppositions made clear) to support the claim made in the first sentence in Table 5.1, an organism cannot simultaneously be human and a reptile. It is possible that the writer of this sentence has some secret knowledge about humans and reptiles and the belief expressed could be justified. To date, however, the "Lizard People" theory – as popularised by David Icke in the late 1990s and espoused by, among others, the Nashville Bomber (Anthony Warner) and, more recently, some Q-Anon adherents – remains a patently untrue theory which owes more to its proponents' antisemitism than to any scientific fact.

Knowledge can only convey information when it is made concrete and articulated through the mind (Stenmark 2002), and background information (explicit or implicit) is required for comprehension of most sentences (Searl 2002). If there is tacit knowledge hidden in the mind of the writer, and it is not expressed coherently, then no information is communicated. As Hodges explains, when analysing the rationality of an argument, facts, premises and agreed beliefs are important:

Table 5.1   Grammatical Sentences with Different Levels of Information Content

	SENTENCE	SEMANTICS	INFORMATION
1	That man, the human next door, he is actually a reptile.	Meaningless	None
2	He murdered that innocent man, but because he didn't really kill him, the victim is dead.	Meaningless	None
3	The sun will "rise" tomorrow.	Hypothesis	Low
4	That tomato you are holding in your hand is a fruit.	Meaningful	High

It seems, then, that in order to assess the rationality of an argument, we need to take into account all the known facts, and not just the stated premises. An argument is normally deployed against a background of known facts and agreed beliefs, and the rationality of the argument depends on what these facts and beliefs are.

(2001, p. 42)

But, even if the belief in the first sentence could be justified, that would not make the statement necessarily true (Gettier 1966). The second sentence could be further clarified but, as it stands, is meaningless (non-information). While the claim in the fourth sentence may appear strange to many people (a tomato is generally thought of as a vegetable) even without support, in the form of clarification within the sentence, the statement is authentic because it is scientifically correct. Stating that a tomato is a fruit is different from saying that the sun will rise tomorrow. The claim in the third sentence is not fact but a hypothesis because what is asserted is really speculation based on historical antecedent (Wittgenstein 1922, p. 10). Information can, therefore, be regarded as the product from data processed through a filter of facts, logic and semantics (see Figure 5.1).

Imperative (or instructional) content contains no propositions. Such content differs from declarative content because it cannot be analysed as true or false. Truth and falsity can only be found in propositions. In Figure 5.1, instructional content would only be checked for logic/coherence and semantic issues but would not be fact-checked.

In light of the ways in which technology, social media, web-based media and the internet generally have resulted in massive changes to how swiftly and widely information – both true and false – can spread across the world, we propose that instructional content be analysed using the "harm principle" (Mill 1859) and by the legal system operating where the content is being analysed. In such analysis, moral norms are important but are distinct from legal systems.

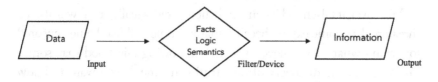

Figure 5.1   A device/filter separating information from data.

Free Speech and the Harm Principle

Free speech is the grey area found somewhere between the pillars of freedom and responsibility. It is recognised as one of the most important tenets of any democratic civil society. Nothing else is more important in a democracy after the establishment of the rule of law. There are, of course, obvious limits to free speech. One cannot shout "fire!" on board a plane or during a crowded session of parliament, for example. Free speech should not cover that type of deliberate recklessness.

How do we draw the limits of free speech? *Can* a government legislate into law what is free speech and what is not? A government, if it has a large enough majority, can muster enough votes in support of such legislation. More pertinently, *should* a government legislate into law what is free speech and what is not? Neither governments nor social media platforms should possess such power. What governments and social media platforms can do is follow universal principles regarding free speech and its limits. One universal principle is the **harm principle** proposed by the British philosopher John Stuart Mill (1859), who proposed that no government or person should interfere and prevent another person's liberty to do or say anything. According to Mill, the only reason that permits interference with another person's liberty is to prevent harm to others.

The Harm Principle 2.0

Mill's "harm principle" is, however, more than 150 years old and in need of an upgrade if it is to remain relevant for the social media age. One such upgrade is proposed by Sunstein (2021, pp. 3–4). Sunstein sides with Mill and believes that free speech should be protected as much as possible for many reasons. Sunstein focuses on misinformation (falsehoods). He believes that both truth and falsehood play important roles in society: arguing that when falsehoods (part of free speech) are censored, we risk a growing tendency for government to censor any speech it does not like.

Moreover, if falsehood is censored, then paradoxically, truth will also be threatened, to some extent, because many people will fear being censored for saying what they believe to be true. Allowing falsehood may sometimes lead to the discovery of new truths in time. If you want to know what people really think and not what they pretend to think, you must make allowance for falsehood. According to Sunstein, the best response to falsehoods is usually to correct them rather than to punish or censor them. Sometimes the result of punishment or censorship is that falsehoods are fuelled still further than might otherwise have been the case. Additionally, there is also the risk that a person may end up feeling so disapproved of and alienated that he/she turns to personalities, groups, chat rooms and forums – such as Reddit, and publications which espouse dangerous, extremist views, many of which have embraced social media and the internet generally – even through apparently innocuous platforms such as popular multiplayer online games (Lakhani 2021) as a means of recruiting new, frequently young and/or vulnerable people to their cause.

By the time parents, educational establishments, governments even, have caught on to the dangers it can be too late. As Farah Pandith (the first-ever State Department special representative to Muslim communities) and Jacob Ware of the Council on Foreign Relations[1] wrote last year:

> When radicalization occurs in the living room and not places of worship and when acts of terrorism no longer require complex planning, barriers to entry are lowered, allowing even teenagers to take active part.
>
> *(Pandith and Ware 2021)*

We only have to look at recent acts of violence by people recruited by the Incel movement (BBC: Incels 2021), ISIS, and far-right organisations such as the Proud Boys and Oath Keepers, among others to see how easily online activity can translate into extreme violence in the real world.

There are limitations to the kind of falsehoods a society should tolerate. Sunstein presents a framework that builds on Mill's "harm principle." But, he is careful to state that:

> …many false statements are not lies; people who make or spread them sincerely believe them to be true. Falsehoods are a broad category of which lies are a mere part. Some people say what they know to be false. Others are reckless; it should be obvious that they are spouting falsehoods, but they do not know it is what they are doing. Still other people are simply mistaken; they had reason to say what they did, but they turned out to be wrong. These differences matter.
>
> *(2021, pp. 3–4)*

These nuances inform Sunstein's framework. The decision to censor or punish falsehood, or to regulate it, must distinguish between four types of peddlers of falsehood or the "state of mind" of the speakers: the liar, the reckless, the negligent and the reasonable. In terms of harm, the magnitude of harm, the likelihood of harm and the timing of harm are all important considerations. How much damage can the particular falsehood cause (grave or moderate or minor or non-existent)? How likely is it that the falsehood will actually cause harm (for certain or probable or improbable or highly probable)? Is the harm from the falsehood immediate, imminent but immediate, or likely to happen in the distant future?

For example, if we look at an event that played out in the full media gaze of the world – the storming of the Capitol on 6 January 2021 by supporters of the outgoing President of the United States, Donald Trump – and the run-up to that day, we can dissect what was said and tweeted by Donald Trump and apply Sunstein's framework. Based upon documents, analysis by law enforcement and the FBI of footage and online activity, and the testimony given by various people to the House 6 January Select Committee – including that by former White House aide, Cassidy Hutchinson, on Tuesday 28 July 2022[2] (PBS 2022) – it is possible to consider whereabouts on Sunstein's framework Donald Trump's various comments, on and offline, fall, according to the evidence available to us currently.

We can see how, at different times, it can be argued that the 45th President engaged in different types of falsehood in Sunstein's framework: Negligent; Reckless; Lie. Whereabouts each of his comments fall will depend on whether or not it can be proved conclusively, or at least argued reasonably, that, at the time of each comment, he knew: that what he was stating publicly was a lie; that what he had stated was more or less likely to result in harm; that he had a reasonable understanding of whether the resulting harm would be minimal or grave; that what he had stated would result in imminent harm or not.

By applying the framework to a recent, real-world event, we can gain a better understanding of the nuances that inform Sunstein's work. It is entirely possible for Donald Trump to have made the same statement at different times and for that statement to fall within a different category based upon how much information he had to hand each time he made that same statement.

Free Speech, Free Reach, Free Expression and Free Impression

Freedom of *speech* online is a human right. Users of social media have the right to make statements, create content and declare their beliefs – if no harm to others is committed. Freedom of *reach* is more complicated: do social media users have the right to get their speech amplified (by the platform's algorithm)? Freedom of *expression* should be guaranteed but not the freedom of *impression* of content upon others if it is harmful.

So, if we return to the above example of President Trump's behaviour and consider his behaviour on Twitter – both in the run up to and during 6 January 2022, and in the immediate aftermath (until his personal Twitter account was permanently suspended on 8th January) – we can see this tension between his right to freedom of *speech* online and his freedom of *reach*. Being able to tweet directly to almost 89 million followers, and for those tweets to be amplified still further as they were picked up and retweeted by other accounts (remember that research from earlier about Twitter cascades and truthful/untruthful statements?), and also covered by other forms of media, enabled one person to spread inflammatory, untrue statements to a far greater audience than would have been the case had he had nothing other than print media and televisual platforms available to him.

Twitter's actions, suspending the @realDonaldTrump account and removing tweets made by President Trump/on his behalf via the official @POTUS, @WhiteHouse, other Government accounts, and Team Trump Twitter accounts, were made because Twitter recognised that by using these other accounts President Trump was attempting to evade his suspension and continue to tweet content that was likely to incite violence[3] (Twitter 2021). And by so doing, it can be argued, attempting to continue to take advantage of the far, far greater *reach* available to him in comparison with most other people at that time.

The Misinformation Challenge

The multifaceted nature of the challenge presented by misinformation requires varied initiatives and solutions. An *infodemiological approach* to misinformation analysis makes use of network analysis. Put simply, this approach seeks to understand the spread of misinformation the way an epidemiologist studies disease (Freedman 2020). Some analysts use a *cybersecurity approach*: viewing online misinformation as a national security challenge. Equipped with cybersecurity tools, they track misinformation the way they would track malware, to prevent "the hacking of people's beliefs" (Kehrt 2020).

A *linguistic approach* to misinformation analysis focuses on the language style of textual claims to assess the credibility of emerging claims online (Popat et al. 2017). For example, is the way the language of a text written by an apparent native speaker similar to that of other native speakers? Does it use idioms and phrases that should be familiar in a believable way? Does the apparently idiosyncratic way of writing by one person appear numerous times by other supposed different and unrelated individuals, thus suggesting the use of bots to spread a particular belief as fact?

Increasingly important is the *social justice/critical theory approach* to online misinformation analysis (Noble 2018; Kreiss 2021; Marwick et al. 2021). This approach emphasises the role power differentials within society play in certain kinds of disinformation that amplify racial stereotypes and increase xenophobia, misogyny and antisemitism. A *social network approach* emphasises that misinformation persists because of social factors that inform belief, as opposed to just individual psychology (O'Connor and Weatherall 2019).

Our *Wittgensteinian approach* to misinformation analysis is based on "analysis" or analytical thinking, which can be differentiated from "criticism" or critical thinking. Analysis involves the decomposition of information to simpler elements for clarity and better understanding, the opposite of "synthesis," whereas critical thinking is more focused on the evaluation of information, interpreting it and making an informed judgement. Cook et al. (2018) present a *critical thinking approach* to deconstructing misinformation. They identify reasoning fallacies, based on argument structure, to refute common misinformation about climate change espoused by denialists. This approach is comprehensive and was successful when applied to 42 claims commonly peddled by denialists.

Analytical and critical approaches complement each other. Misinformation online manifests in different forms. It makes sense, therefore, that a combination of different approaches to tackle it is required for effective solutions.

A Systems Approach to Misinformation Analysis

Breaking down arguments into "logical atoms" (a form of reduction-ism) will not be effective for complex phenomena like conspiracy theories. Analysing conspiracy theories is best done using a *systems approach* or systems thinking (Ammara et al. 2020). Systems think-ing is a way of viewing the world in all its complexity: a holistic (as opposed to reductionist) worldview that emphasises learning and the search for high-leverage points to facilitate lasting positive change (Sterman 2002; Omoregie 2017). As Sterman (2002) shows, the sys-tems approach is not a linear approach or "open-loop, event-oriented view of the world" but rather a "feedback view of the world," also explained by the Waters Foundation (2020). The Waters Foundation describes the following "Habits of Systems Thinkers":

> 1. Seek to understand the big picture; 2. Observe how elements within the system change over time, generating patterns and trends; 3. Recognize that a system's structure (elements and interactions) generates behaviour; 4. Identify the circular nature of complex cause-and-effect relationships; 5. Surface and test assumptions; 6. Change perspective to increase understanding; 7. Consider an issue fully and resist the urge to come to a quick conclusion; 8. Consider how mental models affect current reality and the future; 9. Use understanding of system structure to iden-tify possible leverage actions; 10. Find where unintended conse-quences emerge; 11. Recognize the impact of time delays when exploring cause-and-effect relationships; 12. Check results and change actions if needed: "successive approximation."
>
> *(2020)*

A systems approach to analyse misinformation aims to identify root causes, provide actionable insights and anticipate possible long-term consequences. For example, Ammara et al. (2020) revealed that incor-rect labelling of news by fact-checkers could lead to more scepti-cism of news credibility. They also discovered that too much focus on improvements in artificial intelligence (AI) for detection of fake news could lead to similar technology being used to generate more misinformation.

Misinformation and Malinformation

A quick search on Wikipedia for the entry on "Misinformation" will produce a write up that begins with a definition:

> Misinformation is false, inaccurate, or misleading information that is communicated regardless of an intention to deceive. Examples of misinformation are false rumors, insults, and pranks. Disinformation is a subset of misinformation that is deliberately deceptive.

We like this definition of "misinformation" as the umbrella term for falsehood. However, increasingly popular is the definition that separates disinformation from misinformation (rather than keeping it as a subset of misinformation), and separates the deliberate sharing of false knowledge from that of sharing real information when both are done so for nefarious reasons, such as that popularised by the scholars Wardle and Derakhshan (2017):

> Misinformation is when false information is shared, but no harm is meant. Disinformation is when false information is knowingly shared to cause harm. Malinformation is when genuine information is shared to cause harm, often by moving information designed to stay private into the public sphere.

Dictionary.com named "misinformation" its 2018 "Word of the Year" and explains why "misinformation" is falsehood spread regardless of intention:

> Misinformation is false information that is spread, regardless of intent to mislead… Misinformation doesn't care about intent, and so is simply a term for any kind of wrong or false information… Misinformation is, of course, related to the verb misinform, which means 'to give wrong or misleading information to' and is first recorded around 1350–1400. You'll notice that misinform, like misinformation, also makes no mention of why this wrong information is being spread around, only that it is.

(2021)

So, misinformation is false or misleading information not necessarily intended to deceive; disinformation (false and misleading information with intention to deceive); and malinformation (authentic information with intent to cause harm): all three are common types of information disorders. Disinformation is particularly insidious as it can be transformed by social media into misinformation. This occurs, for example, when deliberate nefarious propaganda is released (disinformation) but subsequently shared through social media innocently by people who believe the propaganda to be true (misinformation). An action that is more likely to happen, and then to spread rapidly, thanks to those algorithms we were discussing in chapter 1, helping to create echo chambers online. Highlighting disinformation as a special form of misinformation is important: it's a matter of motive. However, not all falsehoods are lies: falsehood could result from recklessness, a genuine mistake or a deliberate lie (Sunstein 2021 pp. 3–4).

In 2018, UNESCO published a handbook, "Journalism, 'Fake News' and Disinformation: A Handbook for Journalism Education and Training" to help counteract the new and increasingly varied ways in which trusted information is damaged by the information disorder. Among the handbook's modules is one by Wardle and Derakhshan (2017) that explores the formats of misinformation, disinformation and malinformation. It includes the following examples of the three formats to explain the differences between each type of incorrect information, and the different motivations of those involved in spreading the incorrect information online.

1. Examples of disinformation:
   One of the attempted hoaxes of the French election campaign, was the creation of a sophisticated duplicate version of the Belgian newspaper Le Soir with a false article claiming that the presidential candidate Emmanuel Macron was being funded by Saudi Arabia. Another example was the circulation of documents online claiming falsely that he had opened an offshore bank account in the Bahamas. And finally, disinformation circulated via 'Twitter raids' in which loosely connected networks of individuals simultaneously took to Twitter with identical hashtags and messages to spread rumours about the candidate's personal life.

2. Examples of misinformation:

A terror attack on the Champs Élysées in Paris on 20 April 2017 inspired a great deal of misinformation as is the case in almost all breaking news situations. Individuals on social media unwittingly published a number of rumours, including the news that a second policeman had been killed, for example. The people sharing this type of content are rarely doing so to cause harm. Rather, they are caught up in the moment, trying to be helpful, but fail to adequately inspect and verify the information they are sharing.

3. Example of mal-information:

One striking example of mal-information occurred when Emmanuel Macron's emails were leaked just before the run-off vote on 7 May. The emails were regarded as genuine. However, by releasing private information into the public sphere minutes before the standard electoral ban on any coverage immediately ahead of polling, the leak was designed to cause maximum harm to the Macron campaign.

(Wardle and Derakhshan 2018, p. 45)

As we have discussed previously, the person spreading incorrect information is very often doing so because they believe that what they are sharing is correct and truthful. However, as well as sharing content based on rumours and hearsay posted by people trying to be helpful (as in the terrorist attack in the Champs Élysées), people may also be sharing content that has been designed expressly to spread false content (as in the examples of disinformation and malinformation described above), and, however inadvertently, be doing the work of individuals, groups, organisations, and states seeking to destabilise.

Equally worrying is the possibility that those viewing posts shared by their friends, relatives or colleagues, uncertain as to whether or not what they have just read or viewed is true or not, can end up skewing what they see going forward while attempting to do some fact-checking of their own. The very act of searching online for further information that may confirm (or not) the truthfulness of another's post may well result in algorithms directing them towards sites containing increasingly extreme examples of misinformation, disinformation and malinformation.

Most recently, this has been seen repeatedly in the behaviour of those described as "disappearing down the Q-Anon rabbit hole." We all like to believe that we can't be fooled, but it is frightening how easily and rapidly, aided by algorithms and those spreading conspiracy theories (and managing successfully to evade detection by Big Tech (Teh 2021), we can be persuaded that lies are, in fact, the truth. And, don't comfort yourself with the thought that your intelligence and academic achievements can somehow inoculate you from falling for a conspiracy theory online.

While a lower educational level is often one of the factors related to a propensity to believe conspiracy theories, a recent study of 1001 people examining some of the most prevalent conspiracy theories around Covid-19 circulating on social media, 93% of whom held at least a bachelor's degree, revealed that a worryingly high proportion of respondents held moderate or strong beliefs that common Covid-19 conspiracy theories were true. Including the following: Covid-19 is not real – 12.7% moderate belief/23.6% strong belief; there is already a vaccine that will only be released once millions have been infected – 16.9%/47.3%; people were being sprayed and poisoned by "chem trails" – 41.3%/18%; the participant in the study was generally a believer in conspiracy theories – 43.6%/23.6%; Covid-19 and Ebola were created for population control – 54.9%/18.8% (Constantinou et al. 2020).

As the authors of the study point out, even more, disconcerting than the concerning levels of belief in some of the more out-there theories was the fact that the participants in the study were highly educated, with nine out of ten participants having at least a bachelor's degree. And yet, when faced with the emotive, jargon-free, often relatable stories in support of the various theories (especially when set against the scientific, often acronym-filled, dry news reports and interviews that a lot of the time didn't tell a relatable story of what this might mean for an individual, community, or country), even those who would consider themselves to be educated, intelligent, able to discern what was likely to be wholly or mostly true information online were persuaded of one or more conspiracy theories' "truth" (Constantinou et al. 2020).

Off-information and Non-information

In addition to the existing three terms of misinformation, disinformation and malinformation, we propose the terms "off-information" and "non-information" to describe two other variants of information disorder (Omoregie 2021). "Off-information" is information that is meaningful but potentially harmful and cannot be analysed as being true or false. "Non-information" contains no semantic content – it is meaningless and may or may not be harmful (see Figure 5.2).

Of the four sentences below, only sentence (b) would be considered off-information: it is an instructional sentence with potential to cause harm if obeyed. Sentence (a) is meaningful but not realistic, (c) is wrong advice but not misinformation and (d) is meaningless hence non-information (no evidence of extra-terrestrial visitors on Earth yet!):

(a) *Let's eat all the food in every restaurant in this city today.*
(b) *Swallow arsenic when you feel depressed.*
(c) *Do not believe anything a teacher or professor tells you.*
(d) *You should listen to extra-terrestrials from Venus who live in the apartment next to ours.*

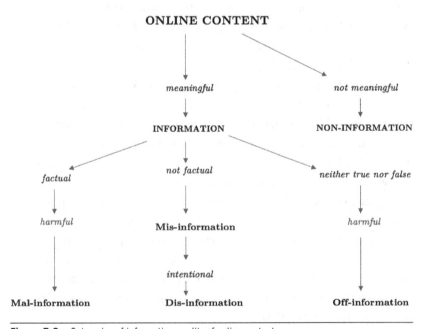

Figure 5.2 Categories of information quality of online content.

Some sentences can be categorised as misinformation *and* non-information: they do not make sense and are false. Frege proposes two distinct aspects of meaning: the sense of the statement and the object to which the statement refers. Truth (or falsehood), according to Frege (1948) is contained in a sentence's reference. Russell (1905) criticises Frege's theory of meaning pointing out that Frege's theory makes no allowance for the fact that some statements refer to objects that do not exist and thus are false statements. For example:

(e) *The present King of France is bald.*

Russell labels the sentence above as "false," or "mis-information," because there is no King of France. We propose that a better category for sentence (e) is "non-information." It is irrelevant whether the King is bald or not because such a King does not exist today. The statement does not make sense. If the King exists, then we could verify if he is bald or not.

Wittgenstein's Approach

About 25 years before Shannon's landmark paper, the Austrian–British philosopher Ludwig Wittgenstein wrote a 75-page tract. Wittgenstein's work, written in the front line of battle, while he served as a soldier during World War I, was submitted eventually to the University of Cambridge as his PhD thesis.

The works of Ludwig Wittgenstein (1889–1951) are usually divided into two: the early and the later philosophy. Wittgenstein's book *Tractatus Logico-Philosophicus* is regarded as his early masterpiece. Another book *Philosophical Investigations* is representative of his later philosophical work. In *Philosophical Investigations* (PI), Wittgenstein refutes important theses he made in *Tractatus Logico-Philosophicus* (TL-P). Great works, however, all too often develop a life of their own, independent of the creator's intentions or vicissitudes.

The results of a 1998 poll of 414 philosophy teachers, in North America (the United States and Canada) revealed TL-P to be among the top five books of philosophy written in the twentieth century (Lackey 1999). The poll requested respondents rank the five philosophy books they rated the highest. The five books with the highest ratings were:

1) 179 *Philosophical Investigations* (L. Wittgenstein, 1953) 68,
2) 134 *Being and Time* (M. Heidegger, 1927) 51,
3) 131 *A Theory of Justice* (J. Rawls, 1971) 21,
4) 77 *Tractatus Logico-Philosophicus* (L. Wittgenstein, 1922) 24, and
5) 64 *Principia Mathematica* (B. Russell and A. Whitehead, 1910) 27.

The number on the left shows the total number of citations (mentions in respondents' top five). The number on the right shows the total number of first-placed rankings (number of respondents who regarded the book as the best of the twentieth century). PI was the clear winner of the poll. TL-P was highly rated: it was regarded by 24 teachers as the best philosophy book of the twentieth century. Not bad for a book that was later described by its author as inadequate, despite the fact that TL-P is a finished work and PI is not (Klagge 2016, p. 48).

Tractatus Logico-Philosophicus (translated as Logical Philosophical Treatise), is about the role facts play in the real world. Wittgenstein declared that facts make up the real world; facts divide the world (draw the boundaries); logic fills the world and limits it such that some issues are better left unsaid as they cannot be analysed properly. We have drawn on Wittgenstein's work for inspiration and guidance in our current misinformation era and posit that a model based on insights from the early philosophical work of Ludwig Wittgenstein could provide a framework for effective online misinformation analysis.

The framework of the early philosophy of Ludwig Wittgenstein (revealed in TL-P) inspired our Global Online Information Quality Check model, for written (non-graphical) misinformation analysis and prevention, as presented in this monograph. In TL-P, Wittgenstein states that philosophy should aim for nothing more than "the logical clarification of thoughts." TL-P is concerned with clarity, the link between thoughts and reality provided by language.

The Key Theses in Tractatus Logico-Philosophicus

TL-P is composed of seven main theses and accompanying remarks (or sub-theses) on these theses. Within the seven main theses,

Wittgenstein tries to get to the heart of the problems of philosophy by explaining how language really works. His theory in TL-P cannot apply to language as a whole, unlike the theory in PI, but, during his ambitious project, Wittgenstein provides insights into the nature of the world of communication and information. In TL-P, we find a useful theory of factual language or discourse, about declarative sentences and propositions, that we find extremely relevant to misinformation analysis and information quality. Some principal theses (relevant to this paper) in TL-P can be summarised thus:

(a) **Facts are the real world**

The thesis number "1" is the first of seven major theses (1–7). Three of its propositions are:

> *The world is everything that is the case.*
> *1.11 The world is determined by the facts, and by these being all facts*
> *1.2 The world divides into facts.*

Thus, according to Wittgenstein, facts divide the world: they determine everything that exists or does not exist in the world. Facts are derived from "states of affairs." States of affairs that exist prove those states that do not exist.

(b) **Language consists of propositions which could represent the world**

> *2.19 The logical picture can depict the world.*
> *3. The logical picture of the fact is the thought.*
> *4. The thought is the significant proposition.*
> *4.001 The totality of propositions is the language.*

For Wittgenstein, the world can be pictured or represented by propositions. Every proposition is either true or false. Language made up of propositions can only represent the world correctly when its propositions are true. A logical picture of a fact is a thought and thoughts find expression through propositions. Every proposition has only one complete analysis and a fact has only one correct analysis. Only factual discourse contains reasoning.

(c) **Logic fills the world and limits it**

Wittgenstein describes the importance of logic in some sub-theses/remarks:

> *5.61 Logic fills the world: the limits of the world are also its limits.*
>
> *6.124 The logical propositions describe the scaffolding of the world, or rather they present it.*
>
> *6.13 Logic is not a theory but a reflection of the world.*

Logic aims to present clearly what can be inferred from a proposition. What cannot be inferred from a proposition is regarded as not valid.

(d) **Some things are better left unsaid and cannot be analysed rationally**

Wittgenstein's last thesis consists of just one line with no sub-theses or remarks:

> *7. Whereof one cannot speak, thereof one must be silent.*

Wittgenstein implies here that certain things/phenomena cannot be properly expressed through language. Instead, they can be described as mystical/mysterious, or simply unsayable. They can be known or shown but not articulated properly. The rules described by Wittgenstein in the preceding six major theses cannot apply to such unspeakable things/phenomena.

In summary, there are four issues in Wittgenstein's Tractatus Logico-Philosophicus that are of relevance to online misinformation analysis: "Facts," "Propositions," "Logic/Analytical," and the "Unspeakable."

All of which leads us onto…

Notes

1 The Council on Foreign Affairs. The CFR is an independent, non-partisan, non-profit American think tank, founded in 1921, that specialises in US foreign policy and international relations. CFR – Council on Foreign Relations. cfr.org

2 Testimony from Cassidy Hutchinson. From 42:03 minutes onwards.

3 In its blog post of Friday 8 January 2022, Twitter explains why it suspended the personal Twitter account of President Trump (@realDonaldTrump) even though he was recognised under its Public Interest Framework as an elected official and world leader whom people had the

right to hear from directly. It takes the reader through the full analysis of the process taken when investigating whether President Trump's tweets of 8 January, relating to the events of 6 January, were in violation of Twitter's Glorification of Violence policy. And explains how and why, in this case, the Glorification of Violence policy outweighs the Public Interest Framework:

> In the context of horrific events this week, we made it clear on Wednesday that additional violations of the Twitter Rules would potentially result in this very course of action. Our public interest framework exists to enable the public to hear from elected officials and world leaders directly. It is built on a principle that the people have a right to hold power to account in the open. However, we made it clear going back years that these accounts are not above our rules entirely and cannot use Twitter to incite violence, among other things.

(2022)

6

THE GLOBAL ONLINE INFORMATION QUALITY CHECK MODEL

The model we propose for online content analysis is a descriptive tool which developed out of our day-to-day online chats and discussions during 2020 (see Figure 6.1). It is inspired by the early philosophy of Ludwig Wittgenstein – whose works Uyiosa had been reading during lockdown – and aims to clarify thoughts and propositions in any content that is analysed. Web-based, written, non-graphical information (such as articles, commentary, etc.) is analysed and then scored, based on criteria designed specifically to evaluate the quality of analytical content.

Post-analysis, the written content is then categorised as "analytical" or "non-analytical." Further labelling of the intrinsic nature of the content (e.g., "satire," "political" and "scientific") and users' (content consumers) ratings complete the process. When applied to web browsers and online social media platforms, we believe, the ratings produced by our model will help users discern content qualitatively and engage more analytically with other users.

At the heart of our proposed solution for how to best check and analyse the quality of online content, without removing the individual's choice of what they choose to read, is the belief that analytical thinking (clarification of thoughts and propositions) is essential for combating information disorder and the lure of echo chambers (Swami et al. 2014). This model applies the four aspects of the Wittgensteinian framework, which are discussed in the next section, consisting of (a) facts, (b) propositions, (c) logical/analytical thinking and (d) labelling unanalysable content.

DOI: 10.1201/9781003308348-6   **63**

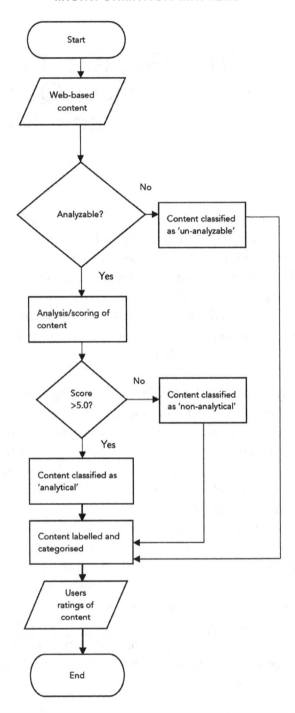

Figure 6.1 Global Online Information Quality Check Model (Global-OIQ).

In our Global-OIQ model, online written content is first fact-checked. The second step is to screen content for propositions and determine whether the content is analysable or not. The third step scores the content as "analytical" or "non-analytical": the score depends on the coherence and logical validity of the content's propositions. The fourth and final step is labelling of the content as a whole. This step is important because conspiracy theories and other such beliefs are not analysed but labelled. Such beliefs are regarded as mysterious, they can only be made manifest or shown and are better left unspoken, in line with the Wittgensteinian philosophy (*Tractatus Logico-Philosophicus* thesis 7, explained in the previous chapter).

Our model is designed deliberately not to endorse or condemn online articles. It upholds freedom of speech. The Global-OIQ model is another tool to help improve the quality of content that people are exposed to online. It is a descriptive tool that builds upon existing tools which fact-check content shared online to provide a more nuanced and in-depth examination of the content. Rather than a free-for-all approach or outright censoring of content, the model takes a middle road that informs the user of the analytical quality of content. As it is our belief that any system that condemns online content outright frequently results in the opposite outcome to that hoped for by those trying to counteract disinformation disorder, users are given a more informed choice whereby they can decide how to label content and how they then interact with that content.

For example, a user could use their own discretion and decide one day that they will only read content with a rating > 7.0 and avoid all "political" content, but the next day focuses on "social commentary" with ratings >3.0. The likelihood of being misinformed, disinformed or malinformed is greatly reduced due to the scoring and labelling system of the model.

The model can improve the quality of discourse and interaction between consumers of online content. Regular use of the model will empower users to scrutinise the level of analytical quality of the content they read. Person-to-person discussions would also be greatly improved. Our hope is that this will help enable people to keep talking and (politely!) arguing with one another, allowing them to better find areas of common ground on which to begin building relationships and ways of working together.

How Does This Analytical Model Work?

All online content can be classified as "analytical" or "non-analytical" based on a list of criteria which include, but are not limited to the following:

1. Are any claims made in the content supported by evidence or are the claims obvious or easily verifiable?
2. Does the content display logical steps in thinking and reasoning?
3. Is the content free of bias and prejudice?
4. Where would the arguments that are presented in the content be placed in Graham's disagreement hierarchy (Graham 2008)?
5. Does the content lean towards conspiratorial or conventional thinking as described by Lewandowsky and Cook (2020)?

Our aim is that monthly trending content on the web (articles, speeches, tweets, etc.) would be researched by Avram Turing and posted on the Global-OIQ's website, ContentQual, as follows:

All analysed content is scored between 0.0 (not analytical) and 10.0 (highly analytical) and then assigned colour-coded badges. Scores between 0.0 and 3.9 have dark grey badges, scores between 4.0 and 6.9 are light grey and 7.0–10.0 scores have clear badges (see Figure 6.2). All content is further categorised and labelled to describe the intrinsic nature of the content:

Content analytical scoring criteria (5 Cs):

Claims: Supports all claims with evidence or claims are obvious/easily verifiable (3.5 points)

Coherence: Displays clear and logical thinking (1.5 points)

Considerate: No bias or prejudice present (1.5 points)

Civil: How civil are the arguments in the content? Where could the arguments be placed in Graham's argument/disagreement hierarchy? (2.5 points)

Conventional: Does the content lean towards conspiratorial or conventional thinking as described by Lewandowsky and Cook? (1 point)

Consumers of content are given the opportunity to rate content already analysed on the ContentQual website. In addition to the

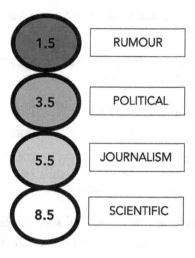

Figure 6.2 Examples of analytical score badges/category labels.

analytical score and content categorisation (labelling), users are asked the following questions concerning the content:

Regardless of whether you agree or not with what is written here, please rate this content in terms of quality of information. Could you cite this content in any discussion? Please rate from *(one star/poor quality) to *****(five stars/recommended reading)

The average user's rating for each content is displayed beside the analytical score and category label. On the ContentQual website, users can browse analysed content and sort them. Content can be sorted by score (higher-scoring content at the top) or by general categories (clicking on "political" lists all trending political content). Users can also suggest other trending content to be analysed and included on the site.

The 50 trending content selected from the web will be analysed monthly and posted on the ContentQual website. The website serves as the database of analysed content for licensed applications to web browsers and social media platforms. Web browser extensions offered to users will show the analytical rating of a trending article, tweet or other content once a link to the content is accessed. Search engines will display search results that include a score for any trending content

Table 6.1   Some Online Articles Analysed using the Information Quality Model

ARTICLE	CATEGORY	LABEL	SCORE
1 DMX Received COVID Vaccine Days Before Heart Attack	RUMOUR	Non-Analytical	2.0
2 Canada Resettled More Refugees Than Any Other Country in 2018	NEWS	Analytical	9.0
3 The NWO, Freemasonry & Symbols on the Dollar Bill	THEORY	Un-Analysable	N/A
4 3100 Inmates to be Released as Trump Administration Implements Criminal Justice Reform	NEWS	Analytical	7.0
5 Race is a Social Construct, Scientists Argue	SCIENCE	Analytical	8.5
6 Ben Carson Says He has No Memory of Running for President	SATIRE	Un-Analysable	N/A

found in the search results. Users of social media platforms like Facebook, Twitter, etc., will see the Global-OIQ score of trending content posted on their newsfeeds.

We Foresee Three Ways of Using Our Proposed Model

First, people could, using the Global-OIQ model as set out below, analyse anything they read online – the "analogue" version, so to speak. Second, monthly trending written content on the web (articles, speeches, tweets, for example) would be researched by Avram Turing and posted on its website. Content that had been selected and analysed would be scored between 0.0 (not analytical) and 10.0 (highly analytical). Third, web browser extensions could be created and offered to users that would reveal automatically the analytical rating of a trending article, tweet or other written content. This rating would be activated once a link to the content was accessed and search engines would then display search results that included a score for any trending written content found in the search results. Users of social media platforms, such as Facebook and Twitter, would see the global analytical quality score of trending content posted on their news feeds (Table 6.1).

Our hope is that these features of the Global Online Information Quality Check Model will encourage the promotion of quality content online and, ideally, as more users become attuned to recognising quality content and discerning its features, they will re-post, re-tweet and forward such content more, leading, over time, to an increase in user engagement with quality content.

7

CONCLUSION

We are living in an information age which has prioritised efficiency over meaning. The twenty-first century's online, public communications platforms were created with the transmission of information being seen as the paramount capability. Information quality was secondary. Moreover, in some ways, it can be argued that although the technology was new, the perception of how it could be used continued to be rooted in older, more traditional ways of communicating news and events with others. There was little consideration given to how an ability to create, share and re-share content almost instantaneously might impact a society that for the most part still believed that the majority of "news" it saw was based on certain facts, even if how those facts were interpreted could change depending on the beliefs of the person, or persons, doing the interpreting.

Add in the fact that we had been told that these new "social" platforms were designed to help us keep in touch and share personal and other news with our friends and colleagues and it is unsurprising that we didn't really comprehend until much later how easy it was to manipulate what we saw and read on these platforms. After all, the early platforms such as SixDegrees, Hi5, Friends Reunited, Friendster, and MySpace; the present-day behemoths Facebook, Twitter, SnapChat, and TikTok; and those such as LinkedIn which span both early and current iterations of online social platforms, all began, and were all "sold" to us, predominantly, as ways of keeping in touch. Of sharing important, funny, heart-warming news. Of being able to network with other professionals. Of finding people who shared the same hobbies as us without being bound by physical geography. Of being able to keep up to date with news and events from around the world.

The idea that our likes, dislikes, friends and group networks, and the information we shared on other platforms: what we bought; what we looked up online; what was written about us both by ourselves and others in online newsletters, business websites, friends' posts on platforms to which we weren't even signed up could all be tracked, collated and stored for perpetuity seemed the stuff of cheesy science fiction. The realisation that as well as enabling us to be directed to fun, innocent things that we were likely to enjoy (stores selling clothes and other items we liked, books by authors new to us, new friends who also liked to garden, or read, or play football, for example) the algorithms used by social platforms might end up ultimately narrowing our view of the world, or taking us to some dark places where small biases morphed into extremist beliefs, came late in the day.

By the time enough of us understood that all was not good in the online Garden of Eden, others had learned how to use these "social" communities for their own purposes. The information disorder had grown, spread, become more virulent. We have been playing catch up with all the misinformation, disinformation and malinformation ever since. And we continue to fool ourselves if we believe the only solution is better, quicker technological fixes: AI that just needs to be programmed better so that it recognises and removes dangerous content from social media platforms. Of course, there is a place for AI and other technological interventions but, again, we need to be aware of the fine line between protecting our freedoms and shutting them down.

We need to acknowledge that we cannot go back to a "golden age" (one that never really existed) where it was easy to understand just by looking at something whether or not it was the "truth." We need to learn for ourselves how to judge more clearly what we are looking at. How to discern whether what is in front of us is more or less likely to be wholly or mostly correct. How to better rely on our judgement rather than assuming that those working for the various platforms will remove "fake news." We need to educate ourselves. We won't make the right call every time. But, so long as we acknowledge that we are still going to be fooled some of the time by what we see, read and hear online, using the Global Online Information Quality Check model goes a long way to placing responsibility for how we interact online back into our hands. And that is not a bad place to be, is it?

Appendix
Detailed Survey Questions and Results

Survey Question 1

How often do you use online social media (Facebook, WhatsApp, LinkedIn, Twitter etc.)?
Every day (95%)
Occasionally/Rarely/Never (5%)

Survey Question 2

What age group do you fit in?
30–49 (49.4%)
50–70 (27.1%)
18–29 (23.5%)

Survey Question 3

Which platform do you typically get most of your news/information articles from?
Google (27.2%)
WhatsApp (23.5%)
Facebook (21%)

Twitter (13.6%)
YouTube/Instagram/LinkedIn (14.7%)

Survey Question 4

When you see news or information forwarded to you, and you are too busy to read it completely, do you sometimes forward the content to someone else after reading only the headline?
Never (39.5%)
Sometimes (32.1%)
Rarely (28.4%)

Survey Question 5

If you encounter information/news/content online that is rated high quality by an independent analyst, would that encourage you to read it?
Yes, I would read it (53.1%)
Maybe I would read it (37%)
I don't know if I would read it (9.9%)
No, I would not read it (0%)

Survey Question 6

If you encounter information/news/content online that is rated high quality by an independent analyst, would that encourage you to forward it?
Yes, I would forward it (34.6%)
Maybe I would forward it (34.6%)
I don't know if I would forward it (18.5%)
No, I would not forward it (12.3%)

Survey Question 7

If you encounter information/news/content online that is rated low quality by an independent analyst, would that discourage you from reading it?
Maybe I would still read it (43.2%)
I would read it (23.5%)
I don't know if I would read it (22.2%)
No, I would not read it (11.1%)

Survey Question 8

If you encounter information/news/content online that is rated low quality by an independent analyst, would that discourage you from forwarding it?
Yes, I would not forward it (40.7%)
Maybe I would not forward it (23.5%)
I could still forward it (19.8%)
I do not know if I would forward it (16%)

Survey Question 9

Have you encountered a website/app that helps confirm how true some information trending online is? Like a fact-checker?
Yes (55%)
No (45%)

Survey Question 10

Do you think a website/app that helps confirm how true information is, like a fact-checker, is important or necessary?
Yes, important (84%)
Maybe important (9.9%)
Not important, not necessary (6.1%)

Glossary of Terms

Algorithm: A set of instructions, a recipe: a step-by-step procedure that takes inputs to process output. These steps are mathematical and are used to process data.

Algorithmic Anxiety: Anxiety connected with the navigation of online platforms whose content is curated by algorithms.

Algorithmic Choice: The concept of giving social media users the choice of algorithms that rate and rank content seen on a social media platform.

Amplification: When online content receives greater than normal engagement by people online due to algorithms.

Analytical: Online content that is logical, coherent and contains claims supported by evidence.

Belief: Subjective acknowledgement of a state of affairs (real or unreal).

Brandolini's Law: An internet adage that posits the amount of effort needed to refute misinformation is of an order of magnitude more than that needed to produce the misinformation in the first place.

Content: Text, images, videos, audio produced online or produced offline and uploaded online which can be shared or circulated.

Content Moderation: Fact-checking or input of additional information or perspective to online content.

Computationalism: An ideology/belief-system that exalts computational process as the central principle or explanation for most human and social experience.

Dataism: Belief that the world today consists of data flows and the intrinsic value of any object or being is the data it holds or brings.

Data void: The absence of credible information from search engines for a particular term, topic or explanation.

Debunking: Fact-check of online content after misinformation exposure.

Digital Literacy: Online skills discerning the distinction between the producers and consumers of news in the digital age which is not always evident. Digital literacy has as its focus online content, the way it is produced, and the special role that user-generated content plays online.

Disinformation: Falsehood online intended to deceive or cause harm.

Dwell Time: Length of time that a thing or person remains in a given state (chiefly engineering). In the online world, Dwell Time is the length of time a person spends looking at a webpage after they've clicked on a link but before clicking back to the original webpage they were on.

Echo Chamber: Online group where members or visitors encounter and reinforce beliefs or opinions similar to what they already believe in.

Extended Mind: Thesis that external artefacts like notebooks, smartphones and computers are part of the human cognitive system.

Fact: Objective state of affairs generally believed and supported with evidence.

Filter Bubble: Similar to echo chamber, but the reinforcement of beliefs is influenced by the algorithmic selection of content by an online platform.

Friction: Measures put in place by online platforms to prevent or slow down the amplification of content.

Harm Principle: Belief or policy that human expression or speech should not be censored if it does not cause harm to another human being.

Infodemic: The glut of problematic content online especially on social media platforms.

Information: Data or content that is well-formed and meaningful.

Information Literacy: Analytical and critical thinking skills for accessing, evaluating and making judgement about new information – especially information found online.

Malinformation: Authentic information, usually private, made public with the intent to cause harm.

Media Literacy: Awareness that the distinct ideological or commercial agenda of some news media organizations could influence how they report or produce news.

Misinformation: False information not necessarily intended to cause harm.

News Literacy: Describes how citizens in democratic societies engage with news, recognizing that objective reporting of news may require value judgements.

Non-information: Meaningless content online which could be problematic.

Off-information: Content that is neither true nor false but harmful.

Opinion: Expression online that can belong to anyone without any consideration of belief, truth or fact and it is always subjective.

Philosophy of Information: Enquiry into technological and informational frameworks within which people make sense of the world today.

Pragmatism: Philosophical approach that prioritises the success and practical applications of belief and opinion through analysis of truth and meaning.

Prebunking: Or inoculation. This involves exposing the flawed argumentation techniques of misinformation to prepare online content consumers against future misinformation.

Tiplines: Fact-checks for content found on platforms with end-to-end encryption like WhatsApp. This solution uses crowd-sourced "tiplines" that contain "tips" submitted by users of a platform (when they encounter a forwarded message containing problematic content) that they feel should be fact-checked.

Semantics: Meaning implied by text: how words, phrases and sentences relate to the world.

Syntax: Sequencing/arrangement of words to produce well-formed sentences.

Truth: State of affairs believed. Less subjective than an opinion and can be personal or generally believed by a group of people. Closely related to fact.

Bibliography

Acerbi A., et al. 2022. Fighting misinformation or fighting for information? *Misinformation Review*. [accessed 2022 August 24] https://misinforeview.hks.harvard.edu/article/research-note-fighting-misinformation-or-fighting-for-information/

Allington D. 2021. Personal communication with Uyiosa Omoregie.

Ammara U., Bukari H., Qadir J. 2020. Analyzing misinformation through the lens of systems thinking. *Proceedings of the 2020 Annual Conference for Truth and Trust Online (TTO 2020)*; October 16–17; Online: Truth & Trust Online. pp. 55–63.

Anscombe G. 1959. *An Introduction to Wittgenstein's Tractatus*. London: Hutchinson & Co. p. 19.

Anstead A. 2021. *Fake News*. London: Sage.

Bak-Coleman J.B., Alfano M., Barfuss W., Bergstrom C.T., Centeno M.A., Couzin I.D., Donges J.F., Galesic M., Gersick A.S., Jacquet J., Kao A.B. 2021. Stewardship of global collective behaviour. *Proceedings of the National Academy of Sciences of the United States of America*. 118 (27). doi: 10.1073/pnas.2025764118

Baker M. 2001. *The Atoms of Language: The Mind Hidden Rules of Grammar*. New York: Basic Books. p. 3.

Baly R., Karadzhov G., Alexandrov D., et al. 2018. Predicting factuality of reporting and bias of news media sources. ar Xiv: Cornell University. [accessed 2020 January 17] https://arxiv.org/abs/1810.01765

Bates M. 1995. Models of natural language learning. *Proceedings of the National Academy of Sciences of the United States of America*. 92. pp. 9977–9982.

BBC News. 2019. Canada resettled more refugees than any other country in 2018. [accessed 2021 February 15] https://www.bbc.com/news/world-us-canada-48696974

BBC News. 2021. Incels: Inside a dark world of online hate. [accessed 2022 June 26] https://www.bbc.co.uk/news/blogs-trending-44053828

Beaney M. 2014. Analysis. *The Stanford Encyclopedia of Philosophy (Summer 2021 Edition)*. [accessed 2021 September 13] https://plato.stanford.edu/entries/analysis/

Bickert M. 2020. Testimony of Monika Bickert Vice President for Global Policy Management, Facebook. Given at The United States House of Representatives January 8 2020. *Hearing Before The United States House Of Representatives*

Committee On Energy & Commerce Subcommittee On Consumer Protection & Commerce. Washington, DC (US) [accessed 2021 October 27] https://docs. house.gov/meetings/IF/IF17/20200108/110351/HHRG-116-IF17-Wstate-BickertM-20200108.pdf

Black M. 1971. *A Companion to Wittgenstein's 'Tractatus'*. London: Cambridge University Press. p. 7.

Boole G. 1952. *Studies in Logic and Probability*. London: Watts & Co. p. 273.

Borowitz A. 2016. Ben Carson says he has no memory of running for president. *The New Yorker*. [accessed 2021 October 17] https://www.newyorker.com/humor/borowitz-report/ben-carson-says-he-has-no-memory-of-running-for-president

Brashier N., Pennycook G., Berinsky A., et al. 2021. Timing matters when correcting fake news. *Proceedings of the National Academy of Sciences 2021*. 118(5). e2020043118. [accessed 2020 August 3. https://www.pnas.org/doi/full/10.1073/pnas.2020043118

Brock A. and Amrute, S. 2020. On race and technoculture [Transcript]. *Databite No.132. Data & Society*. https://datasociety.net/wp-content/uploads/2020/06/On_Race_and_Technoculture.pdf

Brown T., et al. 2020. Language models are few-shot learners. arXiv: Cornell University. [accessed 2020 September 28] https://arxiv.org/pdf/2005.14165.pdf

Buolamwini J., Gebru T. 2018. Gender shades: Intersectional accuracy disparities in commercial gender classification. *Proceedings of Machine Learning Research. Conference on Fairness, Accountability, and Transparency*; February 23–24; New York University NYC. 81. pp. 1–15. [accessed 2022 February 5] http://proceedings.mlr.press/v81/buolamwini18a/buolamwini18a.pdf

Business Standard. 2021. After Facebook, Twitter removes Trump's tweets on us Capitol protests. [accessed 2021 May 27] https://www.business-standard.com/article/international/after-facebook-twitter-removes-trump-s-tweets-on-us-capitol-protests-121010700154_1.html

Carnap R. 1937. *Logical Syntax of Language*. London: Kegan, Paul, Trench, Trubner & Co Ltd. p. 2.

Carnap R., Bar-Hillel Y.. 1952. An outline of a theory of semantic information. *Research Laboratory of Electronics. Massachusetts Institute of Technology. Technical Report No. 247*. [accessed 2020 May 5] https://dspace.mit.edu/handle/1721.1/4821

CERN. 2022. A short history of the web. [accessed 2021 December 19] https://home.cern/science/computing/birth-web/short-history-web

Chalmers D. 2022. *Reality+: Virtual Worlds and the Problems of Philosophy*. New York: Norton & Company.

Chayaka K. 2022. The age of algorithmic anxiety. *The New Yorker*. [accessed 2022 August 25] https://www.newyorker.com/culture/infinite-scroll/the-age-of-algorithmic-anxiety/amp

Chomsky N. 1957. *Syntactic Structures*. Berlin: Mouton de Guyter. p. 49.

Chomsky N. 2017. The Galilean challenge: Architecture and evolution of language. *Journal of Physics: Conference Series*. 880: 012015 1–7. [accessed 2021 September 12] https://iopscience.iop.org/article/10.1088/1742-6596/880/1/012015

Chomsky N. 2021. Personal communication with Uyiosa Omoregie.

Clark A., Chalmers D. 1998. The extended mind. *Analysis*. 58:(1): 7–19.

Clegg N. 2021. You and the algorithm – It takes two to tango. https://nickclegg.medium.com/you-and-the-algorithm-it-takes-two-to-tango-7722b19aa1c2

Constantinou M., Kagialis A., Karekla M. 2020. Preprint. COVID-19 scientific fFacts Vs. conspiracy theories: 0 – 1: Science fails to convince even highly educated individuals. 10.21203/rs.3.rs-33972/v1. [accessed 2021 May 15] https://www.researchgate.net/publication/342023260_COVID-19_Scientific_Facts_

Vs_Conspiracy_Theories_0_-_1_Science_Fails_to_Convince_Even_Highly_Educated_Individuals

Conway F., Siegelman J. 2006. Dark hero of the information age: In *Search of Norbert Wiener the Father of Cybernetics*. New York: Basic Books. pp. 191–195.

Cook J., Ellerton P., Kinkea, D. 2018. Deconstructing climate misinformation to identify reasoning errors. *Environmental Research Letters*. 13(2): 024018; [accessed 2022 August 31]. https://iopscience.iop.org/article/10.1088/1748-9326/aaa49f

Cook J., Lewandowsky S., Ecker U., et al. 2017. Neutralizing misinformation through inoculation: Exposing misleading argumentation techniques reduces their influence. *PLoS One*. 12(5): e0175799.

Darnton R. 2017. The true history of fake news. *The New York Review of Books* [accessed 2020 May 26] https://www.nybooks.com/daily/2017/02/13/the-true-history-of-fake-news/

Davis M. 2012. *The Universal Computer: The Road from Leibniz to Turing*. Boca Raton, FL: CRC Press, p. 12.

Debest T. 2021. Personal communication with Uyiosa Omoregie.

Del Vicario M., Bessi A., Zollo F., et al. 2016. The spread of misinformation online. *Proceedings of the National Academy of Sciences*. 113: 554–559.

Demopoulos W. 1994. Frege and the rigorization of analysis. *The Journal of Philosophical Logic*. 23: 225–245.

Dictionary.com. 2021. "Misinformation" vs. "disinformation" get informed on the difference. [accessed 2021 November 22] https://www.dictionary.com/e/misinformation-vs-disinformation-get-informed-on-the-difference/

Does J., Stockhof M. 2020. Tractatus, application and use. *Open Philosophy*. 3: 770–797

Donovan J. 2020. Social-media companies must flatten the curve of misinformation. *Nature*. [accessed 2020 December 29] https://www.nature.com/articles/d41586-020-01107-z

Dorsey J. 2020. Testimony of Jack Dorsey, Chief Executive Officer Twitter Inc. 2020. Given at the United States Senates Judiciary Committee November 17 2020. Hearing before the United States Senate Committee on the Judiciary. Washington, DC (US) [accessed 2021 October 9] https://www.judiciary.senate.gov/download/dorsey-testimony

Eisenstein E. 1980. *The Printing Press as an Agent of Change*. Cambridge, MA: Cambridge University Press.

Everaert M., Huybregts M., Chomsky N., et al. 2015. Structures, not strings: Linguistics as part of the cognitive sciences. *Trends in Cognitive Science*. 19(2): 729–743.

Facebook. 2021. Facebook news feed – an introduction for content creators. [accessed 2021] https://www.facebook.com/business/learn/lessons/facebook-news-feed-creators

Floridi L. 2019. Semantic conceptions of information. *The Stanford Encyclopedia of Philosophy*. [accessed 2020 August 30] https://plato.stanford.edu/entries/information-semantic/

Floridi L., Chiriatti M. 2020. GPT-3: Its nature, scope, limits and consequences. *Minds and Machines*. 30: 681–694.

Freedland J. 2020. Disinformed to death. *The New York Review of Books*. [accessed 2020 September 27] https://www.nybooks.com/articles/2020/08/20/fake-news-disinformed-to-death

Freedman D. 2020. As QAnon conspiracy theories draw new believers, scientists take aim at misinformation epidemic, *Newsweek*. [accessed 2020 November 5] https://www.newsweek.com/2020/10/23/qanon-conspiracy-theories-draw-new-believers-scientists-take-aim-misinformation-pandemic-1538901.html

Frege G. 1948. Sense and reference. (1892). *The Philosophical Review*. 57(3): 209–230. doi: 10.2307/2181485.

Frege G. 1959. The thought: A logical inquiry. *Mind*. 65(259): 289–311.

Gannon M. 2016. Race is a social construct, scientists argue. *Scientific American*. [accessed 2020 July 1] https://www.scientificamerican.com/article/race-is-a-social-construct-scientists-argue/

Gehl R. 2014. *Reverse Engineering Social Media: Software, Culture, and the Political Economy of New Media Capitalism*. Philadelphia, PA: Temple University Press.

Gettier E. 1966. Is justified true belief knowledge? *Analysis*. 23: 121–123.

Golebiewski M., Boyd D. 2019. Data voids: Where missing data can easily be exploited. *Data & Society*. [accessed 2020 February 18] https://datasociety.net/library/data-voids-where-missing-data-can-easily-be-exploited/

Golumba D. 2009. *The Cultural Logic of Computation*. Cambridge, MA: Harvard University Press.

Gosnell E., et al. 2022 How behavioral science reduced the spread of misinformation on TikTok. [accessed 2021 August 2] https://irrationallabs.com/content/uploads/2021/03/IL-TikTok-Whitepaper2.pdf

Graham P. 2008. How to disagree. [accessed 2020 April 3] http://www.paulgraham.com/disagree.html

Grayling A. 2001. *Wittgenstein A Very Short Introduction*. Oxford: Oxford University Press.

Hammer E. 1998. Semantics for existential graphs. *Journal of Philosophical Logic*. 27(5): 489–503

Harari Y. 2017. *Homo Deus: A Brief History of Tomorrow*. Canada: Penguin Random House.

Hartnett K. 2018. How a pioneer of machine learning became one of its sharpest critics. *The Atlantic*. [accessed 2021 September 16] https://www.theatlantic.com/technology/archive/2018/05/machine-learning-is-stuck-on-asking-why/560675/

Hilbert M., Lopez P. 2011. The world's technological capacity to store, communicate, and compute Information. *Science*. 332(6025): 60–65

Hodges W. 2001. *An Introduction to Elementary Logic*. London: Penguin Books. pp. 12, 17, 42.

Hume D. 2017 (1748). *An Enquiry Concerning Human Understanding*. Whithorn: Anodos Books.

Huzar F., et al. Algorithmic amplification of politics on Twitter, 2021. arXiv: Cornell University. [accessed 2022 January 3] https://arxiv.org/pdf/2110.11010.pdf

Ingram D. 2017. Facebook says 126 million American may have seen Russia-linked political posts. *Reuters*. [accessed 2020 May 4] https://www.reuters.com/article/us-usa-trump-russia-socialmedia-idUSKBN1CZ2OI

James W. 2014. *The Will to Believe. Philosophy of Religion*. London: Routledge. pp. 177–188

Johnson S. 2022. A.I. is mastering language. Should we trust what it says? *The New York Times*. [accessed 2022 August 19] https://www.nytimes.com/2022/04/15/magazine/ai-language.html

Jones-Jang M., et al. 2019. Does media literacy help identification of fake news? Information literacy helps, but other literacies don't. *American Behaviorial Scientist*. 65(2): 371–388.

Kartz Y. 2012. Noam Chomsky on where artificial intelligence went wrong. *The Atlantic*. [accessed 2021 September 8] https://www.theatlantic.com/technology/archive/2012/11/noam-chomsky-on-where-artificial-intelligence-went-wrong/261637/

Kazemi A., et al. 2021. Tiplines to combat misinformation on encrypted platforms: A case study of the 2019 Indian election on WhatsApp, 2021. arXiv: Cornell University. [accessed 2022 January 4] https://arxiv.org/abs/2106.04726

Kehrt S. 2020. One data scientist's quest to quash misinformation. *Wired*. [accessed 2020 September 25] https://www.wired.com/story/data-scientist-cybersecurity-tools-quash-misinformation/

Klagge J. 2016. *Simply Wittgenstein*. New York: Simply Charly. p. 48.

Kreiss D. (Ed. Persily N., Tucker J.) 2021. Social media and democracy: The state of the field, prospects for reform. *International Journal of Press/Politics*. 26(2): 505–512.

Lackey D. 1999. What are the modern classics? The Baruch poll of great philosophy in the twentieth century. *The Philosophical Forum*. 30: 329–346.

Lakhani S. 2021. Video gaming and (violent) extremism: An exploration of the current landscape, trends, and threats. *European Commission*. [accessed 2022 April 14] https://home-affairs.ec.europa.eu/system/files/2022-02/EUIF%20Technical%20 Meeting%20on%20Video%20Gaming%20October%202021%20RAN%20 Policy%20Support%20paper_en.pdf

Leibniz G. 2016 (1714). *The Monadology*. Bolton: Kshetra.

Levitin D. 2020. *A Field Guide to Lies*. Toronto: Penguin. p. xv.

Lewandowsky S., Cook J. 2020. *The Conspiracy Theory Handbook*. Center for Climate Change Communication; George Mason University.

Lycan W. 2019. *Philosophy of Language*. New York: Routledge. p. 73.

Marcus G. 2022. Noam Chomsky and GPT-3: Are large language models a good model of "human" language? [accessed 2022 August 19] https://garymarcus. substack.com/p/noam-chomsky-and-gpt-3

Marwick A., Kuo R., Cameron S., Weigel M. 2021. Critical disinformation studies: A syllabus. Center for Information, Technology, & Public Life (CITAP). University of North Carolina at Chapel Hill. [accessed 2021 April 21] http://citap.unc.edu/ critical-disinfo

McCarthy T. 2020. Zuckerberg says Facebook won't be 'arbiters of truth' after Trump threat. [accessed 2020 June 3] https://www.theguardian.com/technology/2020/ may/28/zuckerberg-facebook-police-online-speech-trump

Michael J. 2021. DMX received COVID vaccine days before heart attack. *Daily Post USA*. [accessed 2022 March 7] https://www.dailypostusa.com/news/ dmx-received-covid-vaccine-days-before-heart-attack-family-says-no-drugs-exclusive/

Mill J.S.. 2010 (1859). *On Liberty*. London: Penguin Classics.

Mims S. 2021. Online speech is now an existential question for Tech. *The Wall Street Journal*. [accessed 2021 March 23] https://www.wsj.com/articles/ online-speech-is-now-an-existential-question-for-tech-11613797254

MIT News. 2001. MIT professor Claude Shannon dies; was founder of digital communications. [accessed 2020 May 6] https://www.newsoffice.mit.edu/2001/ shannon

MIT News. 2018. On Twitter, false news travels faster than true stories: Research project finds humans, not bots, are primarily responsible for spread of misleading information. [accessed 2021 July 14] https://news.mit.edu/2018/ study-twitter-false-news-travels-faster-true-stories-0308

Nature Machine Intelligence (editorial) 2019. Return of cybernetics. *Nature Machine Intelligence*. 1: 385. doi: 10.1038/s42256-019-0100-x.

NewsGuard. 2021. Introducing: NewsGuard. [accessed 2021] https://www.news guardtech.com/how-it-works/

Noble S. 2018. *Algorithms of Oppression: How Search Engines Reinforce Racism*. New York: NYU Press.

Norvig P. 2012. Colorless green ideas learn furiously: Chomsky and the two cultures of statistical learning. *Significance 2011*. 9(4): 30–33.

Nussbaum M. 2018. Minimum core obligations: Toward a deeper philosophical enquiry. jamesgstewart.com. [accessed 2020 June 30] http://jamesgstewart.com/minimum-core-obligations-toward-a-deeper-philosophical-inquiry/

O'Connor C., Weatherall J. 2019a. How misinformation spreads – and why we trust it. *Scientific American*. [accessed 2020 April 3] https://www.scientificamerican.com/article/how-misinformation-spreads-and-why-we-trust-it/

O'Connor C., Weatherall, J. 2019b. *The Misinformation Age: How False Beliefs Spread*. New Haven, CT: Yale University Press.

Omoregie U. 2017. Management thinking for complex issues: Review of two contrasting perspectives. *Frontiers of Management Research (FMR)*. 1: 96–105. http://www.isaacpub.org/images/PaperPDF/FMR_100020_2017091216050950335.pdf

Omoregie U. 2021. Information disorder online is an issue of information quality. *Academia Letters*. Article 2999. doi: 10.20935/AL2999.

Ovada A. 2022. Bridging-based ranking: How platform recommendation systems might reduce division and strengthen democracy. Harvard Kennedy School. Belfer Centre for Science and International Affairs (US). [accessed 2022 June 1] https://www.belfercenter.org/publication/bridging-based-ranking

Pandith F., Ware J. 2021. Teen terrorism inspired by social media is on the rise. Here's what we need to do. [accessed 2022 May 15] https://www.nbcnews.com/think/opinion/teen-terrorism-inspired-social-media-rise-here-s-what-we-ncna1261307

PBS. 2022. *Testimony of Jan. 6 US House of Representatives Select Committee Hearings - Day 6: June 28*. Washington, DC (US) [accessed 2022 July 3] https://www.youtube.com/watch?v=bC3_VFFJlSY

Pearl J. 2018. Theoretical impediments to machine learning with seven sparks from the causal revolution. arXiv: Cornell University. [accessed 2021 September 16] https://arxiv.org/abs/1801.04016

Pears D. 1969. The development of Wittgenstein's philosophy. *The New York Review of Books*. [accessed 2020 October 20] https://www.nybooks.com/articles/1969/01/16/a-special-supplement-the-development-of-wittgenste/

Peirce C.S. 2020. How to make our ideas clear. *Pragmatism*. London: Routledge. pp. 37–49.

Pennycook G., Epstein Z., Mosleh M., Arechar A., Eckles D., Rand D. 2021. Shifting attention to accuracy can reduce misinformation online. *Nature*. 17: 1–6.

Pennycook G., Rand D., et al. 2019. Fighting misinformation on social media using crowdsourced judgements of news source quality. *Proceedings of the National Academy of Sciences of the United States of America*. 116(7): 2521–2526.

Pinker S. 1994. *The Language Instinct: How the Mind Creates Language*. New York: Harper Collins. pp. 69–72.

Popat K., Mukherjee S., Strötgen J., Weikum G. 2017. Where the truth lies: Explaining the credibility of emerging claims on the web and social media. *Proceedings of the 26th International Conference on World Wide Web Companion*. April 3–7 Perth, Australia. pp. 1003–1012. [accessed 2021 February 17] https://doi.org/10.1145/3041021.3055133

Prnewswire.com. 2018. Dictionary.com names 'Misinformation' 2018 Word of the Year. [accessed 2020 August 5] https://www.prnewswire.com/news-releases/dictionarycom-names-misinformation-2018-word-of-the-year-300755058.html

Quine W. 1951. Two dogmas of empiricism. *The Philosophical Review*. 60(1): 20–43

Ramsey F. 1923. Critical notices, Tractatus Logico-Philosophicus. *Mind*. XXXII: 465–478.

Ramsey F. 2016. Truth and probability. *Readings in Formal Epistemology*. Switzerland: Springer, Cham. pp. 21–45.

Ramsey F., Moore G.E. 1927. Symposium: Facts and propositions. *Proceedings of the Aristotelian Society, Supplementary Volumes.* 7: 153–206.

Russell, B. 1905. On denoting. *Mind.* XIV(4): 479–493. [accessed 2021 November 14] https://doi.org/10.1093/mind/XIV.4.479

Russell, B. 2004. *Sceptical Essays.* London: Routledge.

Russell S., Norvig P. 2010. *Artificial Intelligence.* Upper Saddle River, NJ: Prentice Hall.

Sackur S. (Host) 2021. Alan Rusbridger: Fact v fiction. [Audio podcast episode]. *HARDtalk. BBC.* https://www.listennotes.com/podcasts/hardtalk/alan-rusbridger-fact-v-fiction-nMoEgeqR3SH/

Schapals A. Fake news. 2018. *Journalism Practice.* 12: 976–985.

Searl J. 2002. 'Sneaked' or 'snuck'. *The New York Review of Books.* [accessed 2020 August 1] https://www.nybooks.com/articles/2002/03/14/sneaked-or-snuck/

Selyukh A. 2013. Hackers send fake market-moving AP tweet on White House explosions. [accessed 2022 May 28] https://www.reuters.com/article/net-us-usa-whitehouse-ap-idUSBRE93M12Y20130423

Shannon C. 1937. *A Symbolic Analysis of Relay and Switching Circuits [Thesis].* Massachusetts Institute of Technology (MA). [accessed 2022 April 27] https://dspace.mit.edu/handle/1721.1/11173

Shannon C. 1948. A mathematical theory of communication. *The Bell System Technical Journal.* 27(379–423): 623–656.

Sharot T. 2021. To quell misinformation use carrots not just sticks. *Nature.* 2021(591): 347.

Sipley G. 2021. Receptive reading and participatory restraint in Facebook Groups. *The 22nd Annual Conference of the Association Internet Researchers*; October 13–16

Sirlin N., et al. 2021. Digital literacy is associated with more discerning accuracy but not sharing intentions. *Misinformation Review. Harvard Kennedy School: Shorenstein Center on Media, Politics and Public Policy.* 2(6). [accessed 2022 February 7] https://misinforeview.hks.harvard.edu/article/digital-literacy-is-associated-with-more-discerning-accuracy-judgments-but-not-sharing-intentions/

Snopes. n.d. What is snopes? https://www.snopes.com/

Social Media Today. 2020. Twitter shares insights into the effectiveness of its new prompts to get users to read content before retweeting. [accessed 2020 March 28] https://www.socialmediatoday.com/news/twitter-shares-insights-into-the-effectiveness-of-its-new-prompts-to-get-us/585860/

Soulé M.E. 1985. What is conservation biology? *Bioscience.* 35 (11): 727–734.

Spectralplex. 2022. How much content is uploaded to the internet per second? [accessed 2022 August 20] https://spectralplex.com/how-much-content-is-uploaded-to-the-internet-per-second/

Statista. 2022. Most popular social networks worldwide as of January 2022, ranked by number of active users. [accessed 31 August 2022] https://www.statista.com/statistics/272014/global-social-networks-ranked-by-number-of-users/

Stenmark D. 2002. Information vs. knowledge: The role of intranets in knowledge management. *Proceedings of the 35th Hawaii International Conference on Systems Sciences*; January 7–10; Big Island, Hawaii. [accessed 2021 March 14] https://www.computer.org/csdl/pds/api/csdl/proceedings/download-article/12OmNymjN0R/pdf

Sterman J. 2002. Systems dynamics: System thinking and modelling for a complex world. *Massachusetts Institute of Technology Engineering Systems Division, Working Paper Series ESD-WP-2003-01.13-ESD Internal Symposium 2002.* [accessed 2021 May 17] https://dspace.mit.edu/bitstream/handle/1721.1/102741/esd-wp-2003-01.13.pdf?sequence=1&isAllowed=y

Sunstein C. 2021. *Liars: Falsehood and Free Speech in an Age of Deception.* New York, NY: Oxford University Press. pp. 3–4.

Swami V., Voracek M., Steiger S., et al. 2014. Analytic thinking reduces belief in conspiracy theories. *Cognition*. 133: 572–585.

Teh C. 2021. Big Tech cracked down on QAnon but its followers are still diving into online rabbit holes to connect and spread dangerous conspiracies. *Insider*. [accessed 2022 June 14] https://www.businessinsider.com/big-tech-cracked-down-qanon-followers-finding-rabbit-holes-conspiracies-2021-5?r=US&IR=T

The Guardian. 2022 Putin references neo-Nazis and drug addicts in bizarre speech to Russian security council [video]. [accessed 2022 February 26] https://www.theguardian.com/world/video/2022/feb/25/putin-references-neo-nazis-and-drug-addicts-in-bizarre-speech-to-russian-security-council-video

The Peak Performance Center. 2021. Analytical thinking and critical thinking. [accessed 2021 January 28] https://thepeakperformancecenter.com/educational-learning/thinking/critical-thinking/analytical-thinking-critical-thinking/

Thompson S. 2022. How Russian Media Uses Fox News to Make Its Case. *The New York Times*. [accessed 2022 May 12] https://www.nytimes.com/2022/04/15/technology/russia-media-fox-news.html

Turcio L., Obrenovic, M. 2020. *Misinformation, Disinformation, Malinformation: Causes, Trends, and their Influence on Democracy*. Berlin: Germany: Heinrich Böll Foundation. [accessed 2020 October 22] https://hk.boell.org/sites/default/files/importedFiles/2020/11/04/200825_E-Paper3_ENG.pdf

Twitter 2021. Permanent suspension of @realDonaldTrump. [accessed 2021 January 10] https://blog.twitter.com/en_us/topics/company/2020/suspension.

UNESCO. 2018. Journalism, 'fake news' and disinformation: A handbook for journalism education and training. [accessed 2022 April 4] https://en.unesco.org/node/295873

University of Baltimore/CHEQ. 2019. The economic cost of bad actors on the internet. [accessed 2020 December 5] https://s3.amazonaws.com/media.mediapost.com/uploads/EconomicCostOfFakeNews.pdf

van Heijenoort J. 1967. *From Frege to Gödel: A Source Book in Mathematical Logic 1879–1931*. Cambridge, MA: Harvard University Press. pp. 1–82

Verdegem P. 2021a. Introduction: Why we need critical perspectives on AI. In: Verdegem, P. (ed.) *AI for Everyone? Critical Perspectives*. London: University of Westminster Press. pp. 1–18. doi: 10.16997/book55.a.

Verdegem P. 2021b. Personal communication with Uyiosa Omoregie.

Vosoughi S., Roy D., Aral S. 2018. The spread of true and false news. *Science*. 359(6380): 1146–1151.

Waardle C., Derakshan H. 2005. Module 2. Thinking about 'information disorder': Formats of misinformation, disinformation, and mal-information: UNESCO. [accessed 2022 July 25] https://en.unesco.org/sites/default/files/f._jfnd_handbook_module_2.pdf

Warburton N. 2022. The best books on the philosophy of information recommended by Luciano Floridi. [accessed 2022 August 24] https://fivebooks.com/best-books/luciano-floridi-philosophy-information/

Wardle C., Derakhshan H. 2017. Information disorder: Toward an interdisciplinary framework for research and policymaking. *Council of Europe Report*. [accessed 2020 November 28] https://edoc.coe.int/en/media/7495-information-disorder-toward-an-interdisciplinary-framework-for-research-and-policy-making.html

Waters Foundation. 2020. Habits of a systems thinker. [accessed 2020 December 4] https://ttsfilestore.blob.core.windows.net/ttsfiles/habits-single-page-2020.pdf

Weinberg J. 2022. Philosophers on GPT-3. *Daily Nous*. [accessed 2022 August 19] https://dailynous.com/2020/07/30/philosophers-gpt-3/#chalmers

Wikipedia. Misinformation. [accessed 2020 August 23] https://en.wikipedia.org/wiki/Misinformation#cite_note-2

Wikipedia. Brandolini's law. [accessed 2022 July 3] https://en.wikipedia.org/wiki/Brandolini%27s_law

Wittgenstein L. 1922. *Tractatus Logico-Philosophicus*. London: Paul, Trubner & Co.

Wittgenstein L. 1953. *Philosophical Investigations*. Chichester: Wiley-Blackwell.

Wolfram S. 2002. *A New Kind of Science*. Champaign, IL: Wolfram Media, Inc. p. 1104.

Wolfram S. 2019. Testifying at the Senate about A.I.-selected content on the internet. [accessed 2020 June 13] https://writings.stephenwolfram.com/2019/06/testifying-at-the-senate-about-a-i-selected-content-on-the-internet/

World Economic Forum. 2018. Scientists can lead the fight against fake news [accessed 2020 March 28] https://www.weforum.org/agenda/2018/09/scientists-can-lead-the-fight-against-fake-news/

World Newsstand. 1999. The NWO, freemasonry & symbols on the dollar bill. [accessed 2020 September 14] https://freedom-school.com/dollarbill.html

Yablo S. 2011. 24.251 Introduction to philosophy of language. [accessed 2020 November 14] https://ocw.mit.edu/courses/24-251-introduction-to-philosophy-of-language-fall-2011/pages/lecture-notes/

Zapotosky M. 2019. 3,100 inmates to be released as Trump administration implements criminal justice reform. *The Washington Post*. [accessed 2021 February 7] https://www.washingtonpost.com/national-security/3100-inmates-to-be-released-as-trump-administration-implements-criminal-justice-reform/2019/07/19/7ed0daf6-a9a4-11e9-a3a6-ab670962db05_story.html

Zhang A., Ranganathan A., Metz S., et al. 2018. A structured response to misinformation: Defining and annotating credibility indicators in news articles. *Companion Proceedings of The Web Conference 2018*; April 23–27; Lyon, France. International World Wide Web Conferences Steering Committee (IW3C2). pp. 603–612. https://dl.acm.org/doi/10.1145/3184558.3188731

Further Reading

A Misinformation Prevention Reading List

Presented here is a misinformation prevention reading list. This list is not exhaustive. The emphasis is on insights from foundational and background issues about misinformation online. The importance of critical/analytical thinking skills is also highlighted as pre-requisite for prevention of online misinformation. Also highlighted is content from professionals who work at social media platforms explaining how those platforms rate and rank content. This list is separated into two main categories: popular literature and more advanced literature. The popular literature is divided into books, report/manuals/government documents, papers/articles and blog posts/opinion. Eighty works are listed here, for reading, of which 28 are highly recommended (highlighted with *asterisk). The literature spans roughly 150 years from 1859 (John Stuart Mill's *On Liberty*) to 2021 (Cass Sunstein's *Liars*).

I. Books

1. *L. McIntyre (2018). *Post-Truth*
2. *J. Haber (2020). *Critical Thinking*
3. *D Levin (2020). *A Field Guide to Lies*
4. C. Otis (2020). *True or False? A CIA Analyst's Guide to Spotting Fake News*

5. M. Upson et al. (2021). *Information Now: A Graphic Guide to Student Research and Web Literacy*

6. N. Anstead (2021). *Fake News*

II. Reports/Monographs/Manuals/Government Documents

7. The Peak Performance Center (undated). *Analytical Thinking and Critical Thinking*

8. C. Silverman (2014). *The Verification Handbook: Disinformation and Media Manipulation. European Journalism Center*

9. *C. Wardle and H. Derakhshan (2017). *Information Disorder: Toward an Interdisciplinary Framework for Research and Policy Making.* Council of Europe

10. CHEQ/University of Baltimore (2019). *The Economic Cost of Bad Actors on the Internet*

11. C. François (2019). *Actors, Behaviors, Content: A Disinformation ABC.* Transatlantic Working Group

12. *J. Dorsey (2020). *Testimony of Jack Dorsey Chief Executive Officer Twitter, Inc.* U.S Senate Committee on Commerce, Science, and Transportation

13. Gallup/Knight Foundation Survey (2020). *American Views 2020: Trust, Media and Democracy – A Deepening Divide*

14. *S. Lewandowsky and J. Cook, (2020). *The Conspiracy Theory Handbook. Center for Climate Change Communication*; George Mason University

15. S. Aral (2021). *Social Media at A Crossroads: 25 Solutions from The Social Media Summit @ MIT.* Massachusetts Institute of Technology

16. *K. Couric et al. (2021). *Commission on Information Disorder Report.* Aspen Institute

17. HHS.gov Office of the Surgeon General (2021). *Confronting Health Misinformation: The U.S. Surgeon General's Advisory on Building a Healthy Information Environment*

III. Papers/Articles

18. B. Russell (1946). Philosophy for Laymen. *Universities Quarterly*

19. J. Constine (2016). How Facebook News Feed Works. *TechCruch*

20. S. Noble (2017). Google and the Misinformed Public. *The Chronicle for Higher Education*

21. R. DiResta (2018). Free Speech Is Not the Same as Free Reach. *Wired*

22. R. Gonzalez (2018). Don't Want to Fall for Fake News? Don't Be Lazy. *Wired*

23. *E. Hodgin and J. Kahne (2018). Misinformation in the Information Age: What Teachers Can Do to Support Students. *Social Education* 82 (4), pp. 208–212

24. *C. Wardle (2019). *Understanding Information Disorder.* First Draft

25. W. Sady (2019). "Ludwik Fleck". *The Stanford Encyclopedia of Philosophy.*

26. *E. Zuckerman (2019). Building a More Honest Internet: What Would Social Media Look Like if It Served the Public Interest? *Columbia Journalism Review*

27. *J. Cottone (2020). What Do You Know? Facts vs Truth. *Psychology Today*

28. D. Freedman (2020). As QAnon Conspiracy Theories Draw New Believers, Scientists Take Aim at Misinformation Pandemic. *Newsweek*
29. P. Michelman and S. Aral (2020). Can We Amplify the Good and Contain the Bad of Social Media? *MIT Sloan Management Review*
30. E. Gosnell et al. (2021). How Behavioural Science Reduced the Spread of Misinformation on Tik Tok. *Irrational Labs*
31. K. Hao (2021). How Facebook Got Addicted to Spreading Misinformation. *MIT Technology Review*
32. I. Leslie (2021). How to Have Better Arguments Online. *The Guardian*
33. A. Stark (2021). A Little Humility, Please [Book Review of Rationality by Steven Pinker]. *The Wall Street Journal*
34. J. Taylor (2021). Reddit Defends How It Tackles Misinformation As it Opens Its Australian Office. *The Guardian*
35. *J. Golbeck (2022). Social Media and Shared Reality. *Science*
36. K. Chayaka (2022). The Age of Algorithmic Anxiety. *The New Yorker*

IV. Blog Posts/Opinion

37. *P. Graham (2008). How To Disagree. *Paul Graham*
38. *C. Wardle (2017). Fake News. It's Complicated. *Medium*
39. *D. Boyd (2018). So You Think You Want Media Literacy…Do You? *Data & Society*
40. *C. Meserole (2018). How Misinformation Spreads on Social Media. *The Brookings Institution*
41. *J. Smith et al. (2018). Designing New Ways to Give Context to News Stories. *Facebook*
42. *C. Wardle (2018). Information Disorder: The Definitional Toolbox. *First Draft*
43. *Facebook Help Centre (2021). Tips to Spot False News. *Facebook*
44. *N. Clegg (2021). You and the Algorithm: It Takes Two to Tango. *Facebook*
45. *A. Mantzarlis (2021). Spot Misinformation Online with These Tips. *Google*

V. More Advanced Material

46. D. Hume (1740). *Enquiries Concerning Human Understanding*
47. J. Mill (1859). *On Liberty*
48. G. Frege (1892). Sense and Reference. *The Philosophical Review* 1948; 57 (3) pp. 209–230
49. J. Dewey (1910). *How We Think*
50. L. Wittgenstein (1921). *Tractatus Logico-Philosophicus*
51. L. Fleck (1935). *The Genesis and Development of a Scientific Fact* (A good summary of this book and Ludwik Fleck's philosophy can be found at: W. Sady, "Ludwik Fleck", *The Stanford Encyclopedia of Philosophy*, 2019)
52. L. Floridi (2010). *Information: A Very Short Introduction*
53. D. Cryan et al. (2013). *Introducing Logic: A Graphic Guide*
54. V. Swami et al. (2014). Analytical Thinking Reduces Belief in Conspiracy Theories. *Cognition*; 133: 572–585
55. T. Williamson (2015). Knowledge and Belief. 24.09x Minds and Machines, *MITx (edX)*

56. S. Zuboff (2015). Big Other: Surveillance Capitalism and the Prospects of an Information Civilization. *Journal of Information Technology*, 30(1), pp. 75–89

57. D. Miller et al. (2016). *How the World Changed Social Media*

58. H. Allcott and M. Gentzkow (2017). Social Media and Fake News in the 2016 Election. *Journal of Economic Perspectives*, 31(2) pp. 211–236

59. M. Beaney (2017). *Analytic Philosophy: A Very Short Introduction*

60. A. Marwick and R. Lewis (2017). *Media Manipulation and Disinformation Online.* Data & Society

61. *R. Caplan et al. (2018). *Dead Reckoning: Navigating Content Moderation After 'Fake News'.* Data & Society

62. J. Kavanagh and M. Ritch (2018). *Truth Decay.* Rand Corporation

63. S. Noble (2018). *Algorithms of Oppression: How Search Engines Reinforce Racism*

64. A. Zhang et al. (2018). A Structured Response to Misinformation: Defining and Annotating Credibility Indicators in News Articles. *Companion to Proceedings of the World Wide Web Conference 2018*, pp. 603–612

65. *J. Cook et al. (2019). Deconstructing Climate Misinformation to Identify Reasoning Errors. *Environmental Research Letters.* 13(2): 024018

66. M. Golebiewski and D. Boyd (2019). *Data Voids: Where Missing Data Can Easily Be Exploited.* Data & Society

67. G. Lim (2019). *Disinformation Annotated Bibliography.* Citizens Lab

68. W. Lycan (2019). *Philosophy of Language*

69. *C. O'Connor and J. Weatherall (2019). *The Misinformation Age: How False Beliefs Spread*

70. *S. Wolfram (2019). *Optimizing for Engagement: Understanding the Use of Persuasive Technology on the Internet Platforms.* U.S Senate Committee on Communications, Technology, innovation and the Internet

71. U. Ammara et al. (2020). Analyzing Misinformation Through the Lens of Systems Thinking. *Proceedings of the 2020 Truth and Trust Online*, pp. 55–63

72. *S. Aral (2020). *The Hype Machine: How Social Media Disrupts Our Elections, Our Economy and Our Health – and How We Must Adapt*

73. C. Miller and C. Colliver (2020), *Developing a Civil Society Response to Online Manipulation.* Institute for Strategic Dialogue

74. L. Turico and M. Obrenovic (2020) *Misinformation, Disinformation, Malinformation: Causes Trends and Their Influence on Democracy.* Heinrich Böll Foundation

75. J. Bak-Coleman et al. (2021). Stewardship of Global Collective behaviour. *Proceedings of the National Academy of Sciences of the USA*; 6; 118(27)

76. W. Morris and C. Brown (2021). "David Hume". *The Stanford Encyclopedia of Philosophy*

77. *G. Pennycook et al. (2021). Shifting Attention to Accuracy Can Reduce Misinformation Online. *Nature*; 592, pp. 590–595

78. *S. Pinker (2021). *Rationality: What It is, Why It Seems Scarce, Why It Matters*

79. C. Sunstein (2021). *Liars: Falsehood and Free Speech in an Age of Deception*

80. M. Zurko (2022). Disinformation and Reflections from Usable Security. *IEEE Security & Privacy*, Vol. 20, pp. 4–7.

Index

Pages in *italics* refer figures and pages in **bold** refer tables.

The Global Online Information Quality Check Model is referred to by its acronym: Global-OIQ

Printed in the United States
by Baker & Taylor Publisher Services